A CHATTO & WINDUS PAPERBACK
CWP 34

THE ROMANTIC SURVIVAL

G000245028

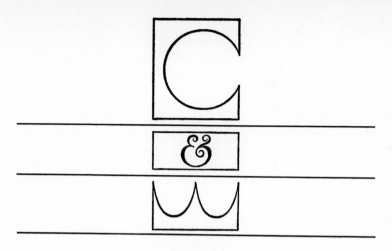

THE
ROMANTIC SURVIVAL

A Study in Poetic Evolution

JOHN BAYLEY

FELLOW OF NEW COLLEGE
OXFORD

CHATTO & WINDUS
LONDON

Published by
Chatto and Windus Ltd.
London WC2

*

Clarke, Irwin and Co. Ltd.
Toronto

First published 1957
by Constable & Co. Ltd.
Reprinted 1958, 1960 and 1964
First issued in this edition 1969

SBN 7011 1492 4

© 1957 by John Bayley

Printed Offset Litho in Great Britain by
Cox and Wyman Ltd
London, Fakenham and Reading

CONTENTS

ACKNOWLEDGEMENTS

For permission to print extracts from copyright poems the author is indebted to the following authors and their publishers: JOHN BETJEMAN (John Murray). T. S. ELIOT: extracts from 'Burnt Norton' and 'East Coker' from *Four Quartets*; and an extract from the essay 'The Metaphysical' from *Collected Essays* (1932) (Faber & Faber Ltd.; Harcourt Brace & Co. Inc.). W. H. AUDEN: extracts from poems nos. 22, 29, 16 and from 'Paid on Both Sides' from *Poems* (1930); nos. 11 and 29 from *Look Stranger* (1940); nos. 5, 8, 20 and 22 and 'Spain' from *Another Time* (1940); from 'The Sea and the Mirror' from *For the Time Being* (1945); extracts from *The Age of Anxiety* (1948); from 'The Fall of Rome', 'Song', 'Memorial for the City' and 'Secrets' from *Nones* (1952); III and No. 29 from *Shorter Poems* (1950) (Faber & Faber Ltd.; Random House Inc.). W. H. AUDEN: extracts from the essay 'Squares and Oblongs' from *Poets at Work* (Harcourt Brace & Co. Inc.). W. B. YEATS: extracts from *The Collected Poems of W. B. Yeats* (Messrs. A. P. Watt; The Macmillan Company). WALTER DE LA MARE: extracts from *Collected Poems* (The Society of Authors; Henry Holt & Co.). DYLAN THOMAS: extracts from his letters written to Henry Treece and quoted in Mr. Treece's *Dylan Thomas* (Henry Treece; Ernest Benn Ltd.; Pearn Pollinger & Higham, acting for the Trustees of the copyrights of the late Dylan Thomas). DYLAN THOMAS: extracts from 'Out of Sighs', 'I in my Intricate Image', 'Especially when the October Wind', 'Before I Knocked', 'Altarwise by Owl-Light', 'After the Funeral', 'Twenty-four Years', 'When like a Running Grave', 'The Conversation of Prayer', from *Collected Poems* (1952) (J. M. Dent & Sons Ltd.; New Directions); and an extract from *Under Milk Wood* (J. M. Dent & Sons Ltd.). WILFRED OWEN (Chatto & Windus Ltd.).

PART ONE

THE
ROMANTIC
DILEMMAS

CHAPTER I

Annex or Survive?

'OUR KING was with us—yesterday', is the lament of Romance's 'chosen bard' in Kipling's poem. Kipling is taking briskly to task those old-fashioned spirits for whom Romance is always located at a distance from the realities of life; for whom distance lends enchantment to the view, and the real longing is always for what is lost or unattainable. He is confident that they are wilfully looking for Romance in the wrong places: it is not an affair of the nostalgic yearning and the backward look, sailing ships, knights in armour and the Golden Age; but it is present here and now, in the street, in the factory, and the grey atmosphere of modern England (the poem appeared in 1894). 'All unseen'—and while its disappearance was being lamented, 'Romance brought up the 9.15'.

To the intellectual of today Kipling's attitude can scarcely seem anything but banal, a painfully jaunty and contrived attempt to reconcile some kind of lyrical vision with the daily grind of an industrial society and a mechanistic view of things. Few of us after a certain age can take very seriously the 'unconsidered miracle' of triple expansion engines, and the Romance of Rivets—especially of rivets who converse with each other; such things seem merely an eccentric offshoot of a decaying plant. For a poet like W. H. Auden the industrial landscape of his childhood was indeed his first love.

3

Better far than any Kings and Queens
I liked to see and hear about machines—

he writes, and he has retained a gift for using the machine in his poetry in several ways. But a more frequent experience of the modern poet seems to be that described by Ronald Bottrall in his poem *The Thyrsus Retipped*.

Power-house stacks, girder-ribs provide a crude base;
But man is what he eats, and they are not bred
Flesh of our flesh, being unrelated
Experientially, fused in no emotive furnace.

Cruder, less concerned with the sensitivity of flesh to metal, Kipling's poem is an affirmation of the durability of Romance in its simplest form—its power of investing ordinary objects with wonder and strangeness, a power still reflected in the popular usage of the term to describe the effects of love. However much we may dislike Kipling's self-confidence, his assertion is remarkably similar to Wordsworth's account of his poetic aims in the Preface to the *Lyrical Ballads*. Wordsworth intends, he says, to choose everyday subjects and 'situations from common life', and to throw over them 'a certain colouring of the imagination in order to present them in an unusual aspect'. And the 'Pylon School' in the twenties and thirties were following the example of Kipling and Wordsworth. Their deliberate attempt to absorb the triviality of the new phenomena into their poetic field may be contrasted with T. S. Eliot's bleak use of such things— gramophones and lost golf-balls play a natural part in the world of his imagery in a way in which the bridges and depth-charges of the Pylon School do not in theirs. The reason may be that Eliot does not acknowledge the Romantic duty of making common objects rich and strange: his

4

classical *O Tempora O Mores* attitude makes no effort to like what it admits to exist. But other modern poets, followers of Wordsworth in this respect, and—ironically enough—of Kipling, attempted to make the new objects 'manifestly and palpably material to us as enjoying and suffering beings', to borrow Wordsworth's phrase. When the process works we get something like Stephen Spender's air-liner:

> *More beautiful and soft than any moth*
> *With burring furred antennae feeling its huge path.*

John Betjeman, though of course belonging to no school and using his material with no theoretical purpose, sings with real delight of the urbanisation of Surrey—

> *Far, far below me roll the Coulsdon woodlands*
> *White down the valley curves the living rail,*

('Southern Electric 25 minutes' appends the author in a helpful footnote.)

As 'enjoying and suffering beings' we can hardly fail to respond to the charm with which these poets invest their material, and their enthusiasm seems precisely of the kind which poets once felt for glamour and romance, with contemporary objects substituted for the moated grange and the ivy-mantled tower. This simple aspect of Romanticism has certainly shown itself to be perennial. But though we have the romantic excitement here, we do not have the romantic authority, that 'universality' which was so often and so uncompromisingly claimed for poetry at the period of the Romantic Revival (we shall reserve a capital letter for the adjective only when using it in this historical context). Indeed it is the absence of authority, the happy and childlike quality of Spender's and Betjeman's approach to aeroplanes and railways, that makes their poetry on these topics so effective. The air-liner becomes a moth, bumbling, furry, and harmless; the adjective *living* seems to admit the electrified railway to a similar place among the inoffensive and vital objects of the human scene: indeed the phrase *living rail*, at one time a railway advertisement slogan, adds a rich satirical overtone to the passage, whose lyrical force takes its origin from a complete acceptance of today's materials, however shoddy and banal these may be.

Can the phenomena of the modern world only be treated in this essentially lightweight way, and turned to favour and to prettiness, or can they be in some way related to a profound and unified vision of human fate and the human soul as Wordsworth and Coleridge related their subject-matter? Can Romance, in fact, still have authority and depth as well as excitement and freshness? Though it can still offer us a new vision of the external world, will this seem to connect swiftly and intimately with the deepest issues of life as does, for example, Wordsworth's vision of the leech-gatherer? This contemporary romantic dilemma is seen in its acutest form in Russia and America, in the poetry of Mayakovsky and Hart Crane. Both made an ambitious and full-scale attempt to absorb the world of machines into the world of man's mental experience, as Wordsworth had sought to absorb the great spectacle of external nature into the compass of the poet's mind. 'Absorb' is the key-word, and Hart Crane employs it when he writes that 'the task of poetry now is to absorb the machine, i.e. to acclimatise it, as naturally and casually as trees, cattle, galleons . . .'. He felt, evidently, that the moment envisaged by Wordsworth had arrived, 'when what is now called science shall be ready to put on, as it were, a form of flesh and blood', and 'the poet will lend his divine spirit to aid the transfiguration'. 'A form of flesh and blood'—Wordsworth's words cannot help reminding us of what Spender and Betjeman did to the air-liner and the railway-line, of what, presumably, Hart Crane is trying to do with Brooklyn Bridge, a structure which he sees as uniting the spirit of man with the created world of his mechanical achievement. ('How could mere toil align thy choiring strings?') Certainly Crane does not fall into the error, as Kipling might well have done had he set out to romanticise the world of the machine on the same ambitious scale, of describing the industrial world for its own sake; he attempts to show how the creative imagination of man controls and harmonises with it, as Wordsworth showed the relationship of that imagination to the world of nature.

But the attempt fails. Crane's feverish brilliancy of language lapses frequently into the merely chaotic, and the reader is uneasily aware of an ideal that hangs unattained before the poet and urges him on to still further futile displays of energy. We see the same process at work in the poetry of Mayakovsky, and both poets committed suicide after lives of extreme disorder and wretchedness largely caused by their unrealised ambitions to hail the greatness of the new industrial society. Their vision had all the old Romantic magnitude, but could not find an adequate poetic form. Like Wordsworth, both felt 'bliss was it in that dawn to be alive' and yet both became 'mighty poets in their misery dead'.

Why did they fail?—or rather, to put the query less baldly, was there any prospect of their succeeding? According to much early Romantic precept, there was; and in order to understand their failure we must glance at the main lines of theory laid down at the beginning of the nineteenth century which have had so much effect on the practice of poetry ever since.

Broadly speaking we can divide early Romantic theory

7

into two parts. The first, associated with Coleridge and Wordsworth in England and Schiller and Goethe in Germany, stresses the sublime and vital function of man's imagination, which gives order and meaning to his surroundings, and of poetry, the imagination's chief instrument of expression. This great power seemed solitary, the great 'I am', 'the dread watch-tower of man's absolute self', the most potent embodiment of the individual self-consciousness; and it is its solitary, isolated nature which provokes the alternative type of Romantic theory—or Romantic awareness rather—which is given by Keats the name of Negative Capability. Keats uses this phrase in relation to Shakespeare, and means by it the ability to enter into all modes of being, animate and inanimate, and to understand and express their nature as it were from the inside. This Romantic polarity is the first of many that we shall encounter, and it turns on the question of the poet's consciousness—is he a solitary Imagination whose function is somehow to absorb the outside world, or is he a mere negative spirit, not a person at all, whose gift it is to elicit reality by penetrating the phenomena of the outside world, 'a very Proteus of the fire and flood'?

Clearly, these roles of the Imagination are complementary, or, if we prefer it, two different ways of looking at the same thing; and this Keats admits as he sets up his concept of Negative Capability as the other half of what he calls Wordsworth's 'Egotistical Sublime'. So does Coleridge, in considering Milton and Shakespeare the two halves of a great imaginative whole. But where the subsequent history of Romanticism is concerned, the first, the theory of the self-conscious Imagination, is by far the more influential. In the case of Hart Crane, it is difficult not to feel that the abstract conception of what he had to do preceded the creative process and so negated it; his poetry is oppressed and inhibited

8

by the task his imagination had consciously set itself. As Keats put it, 'if poetry come not as naturally as the leaves to a tree it had better not come at all', and certainly the absence of any conscious unifying aim, and of any desire to integrate the air-liner or the electrified railway into a vision of life as a whole, makes a great contribution to the success of Spender's and Betjeman's poems. Their capability is of the negative sort, in this context at least: they do not unify, they enter into; but the process is a limited one, and this half of the imagination seems to have renounced the greatness of the Romantic claim.

For that claim was great, and in the writings of the theoreticians of the Romantic Revival it was quite explicit. Coleridge and Wordsworth were intent on transforming the place of poetry in society: from a specialised, agreeable, but not very high-ranking pursuit and taste—like a taste for sherry, as Wordsworth scornfully put it—it was to be given the highest place in human affairs. Shelley called it the visible expression of the Imagination, and the Imagination was 'reason in her most exalted mood'. Poetry was to be no longer a relaxation, and a plaything separated from reason, 'whose use hath been', as Bacon said, 'to give some shadow of satisfaction to the mind of man in those points wherein the nature of things does deny it'. Now the poet's purpose was to reconcile man with his surroundings, and his imagination with what it fed on in the external world.

The poetic imagination was to be one of the chief bridges between the newly propounded categories of the Objective and the Subjective, the individual and his environment. This second Romantic polarity obsesses, in its various forms, the poetry of the nineteenth century: indeed it would be a reasonably safe generalisation to say that the premises on which any romantic poem is written are an acute consciousness of the isolated creating self on the one hand, and of a world unrelated, and possibly uninterested and hostile, on the other; and the wish somehow to achieve a harmonious synthesis of the two. 'The modern conception of art', says Baudelaire, 'is to create a suggestive magic including at the same time object and subject, the world outside the artist and the artist himself'. Coleridge's awareness of the subject object distinction was so obsessive that his notebooks are full of remarkable ideas for poems in which he proposes to treat, 'in a metaphysical manner', the interplay between his mind and some external object, like a patch of snow on the mountain-side which looked 'like a tree or seaweed'. He wished to describe the 'forms' of the mountain seizing him as he looked at them and making a ghost of him and the mountain 'real' until he had reconquered his substance. This exchange of personalities reminds us of Keats's idea of Negative Capability and the account in his letters of taking part in the life of the sparrow that picks about on the gravel outside his window. But whereas Keats's participation is instinctive and unrehearsed, expressing itself in poetry as naturally as the bird does in its movements, Coleridge's curiosity is analytic —what fascinates him is the nature of his own mental and creative process. And this is probably why the poem he projected on the idea was never written.

The legacy of the Romantic Revival came rather from Coleridge than from Keats, and its embarrassments were in some ways crippling. Self-consciousness and responsibility were the two prime entails—the self-consciousness of the poet about how and why he wrote poetry, the responsibility of the poet towards the new duties which Romanticism had laid on him. And these, as we have seen, were not light. True, if the status of poetry had been elevated and its sphere enlarged, few people were aware of the fact: ironically enough it was Byron, whose views on poetry approximated closely to those of the eighteenth century, who of all the Romantics most impressed the popular imagination, and this he did as a personality rather than as a poet. But if the public remained unaware of the implications of what Coleridge and Wordsworth had done, the poet did not.

> *These, these will give the world another heart*
> *And other pulses. Hear ye not the hum*
> *of mighty workings?*

So Keats writes of the great spirits of the Revival in his second sonnet to Haydon. Shelley proclaimed poets to be 'the unacknowledged legislators of the world', and Wordsworth had written in the letter to Lady Beaumont that 'to be incapable of a feeling of poetry, in my sense of the word, is to be without love of human nature and reverence for God'. The poet might indeed feel that the cares of the world were on his shoulders.

Keats did feel it, and his work on Hyperion was almost certainly inhibited by the fear that he was not writing a poem in which humanity, 'the agonies, the strife of human hearts' would be adequately experienced and represented. Tennyson, in *The Palace of Art*, reveals a guilty romantic conscience: an eighteenth-century poet would have been astonished by the idea of 'sharing' artistic talent with the world at large—one had it, and one's friends enjoyed it, and there was an end of the matter. And yet Tennyson, with the aid of Lamarck and Cuvier and his own intuitive convictions, wrestled by no means so unsuccessfully as is sometimes thought to subdue the demons of science and evolution and bring them into the fold. Meanwhile, Matthew Arnold, although protesting against 'the strange disease of modern life', strove to show that poetry was a prime agent in the campaign for sweetness and light which he continued to wage amid the growing darkness and degradation of the Victorian scene. Both he and Tennyson became more and more aware of the difficulties of their task. The rift between their values and the values of the society for whom they wrote was always growing wider—how was 'the still sad music' of Victorian humanity to be brought into poetry? And in both poets there is a corresponding discrepancy between their poetic voice and their prose voice. Tennyson's forceful unofficial utterances are famous. His official vision of the mystery and beauty of procreation at the end of *In Memoriam* may be set against his explosion of slightly comic horror at the leaping Victorian birthrate—'lavish profusion terrifies me—the torrent of babies!—and fifty may die if one survives'. In some sense the near-sublimity of the *In Memoriam* ending is let down by the poet's other and more incisive vision.

In Arnold's poetry the concept of 'high seriousness' identifies itself in practice with an Homeric ideal of dignity and form not ideally suited to the 'Criticism of Life' which, in orthodox Wordsworthian tradition, he held that poetry should be. This seriousness, and the air of dignified depression that overhangs Arnold's verse, are in remarkable contrast with the bitter and sardonic polish of his prose style. It is impossible to conceive of Wordsworth and Coleridge writing their prose and their poetry on two such different levels; indeed one of the most remarkable features of the early Romantics is the homogeneous tone of their poetry and prose—we have only to compare the tone of Keats's letters with *Sleep and Poetry*, or think of Coleridge's notebooks and the famous prose glosses to the *Ancient Mariner*. We must return to this in the next section, but the point to notice now is that the grand idea of poetry as an all-embracing and unifying influence, irrespective of technical forms, had already been tacitly given up. Before ugliness and *Philistinism* (Arnold's new-coined word) the Romantic Imagination was in retreat. It found itself unable to contain and absorb such things, even to the extent in which Wordsworth, in *The Excursion,* had contrived to absorb and subsume under his imaginative control the nocturnal activity of a cotton-mill beside the moorland stream. He has annexed the factory, somehow, to his vision of society as a whole, and can talk about it in the same breath as nature and man's heart. Though deploring the effect of 'the many-windowed fabric huge' on the family life and traditions of its employees,

> *yet do I exult* (he goes on)
> *Casting reserve away, exult to see*
> *An intellectual mastery exercised*
> *O'er the blind elements; a purpose given;*
> *A perseverance fed; almost a soul*
> *Imparted, to brute matter.*

A masterful attempt at romantic ingestion! It was one which few other nineteenth-century poets dared to make. Where Wordsworth's imagination had seized on, transformed, and annexed to poetry the Idiot Boy, Alice Fell, and Martha Ray of *The Thorn,* Matthew Arnold, reading an account of a poor girl in a newspaper, could see only the appalling ugliness of brute fact. Concerning the girl, who like the woman in *The Thorn* was suspected of murdering her child (one wonders whether Arnold perceived the similarity) there was only the bleak announcement: 'Wragg is in custody'. 'Wragg is in custody!' exclaims Arnold. 'The sex lost in the confusion of our unrivalled happiness, and the Christian name lopped off by the straightforward vigour of our

Anglo-Saxon breed!' And what a name besides, he goes on, what can be expected, what can be hoped, of people with such names and of a country that can give them! Beneath his satiric distaste there is a kind of basic misanthropy in Arnold's reaction, a pessimism that does not seem so different from Swift's disgust with human ugliness and folly. As Reason failed Swift and led him finally to his grotesque parable of the Houynhmns, the horses who alone were rational creatures, so the Imagination had failed Arnold. It could no longer interpenetrate and illuminate such a situation as it had done for Wordsworth.

> *At all times of the day or night*
> *The wretched woman thither goes*
> *And she is known to every star*
> *And every wind that blows.*
> *And there beside the thorn she sits*
> *While the blue daylight's in the skies.* . . .

But Wragg had no such words said over her to bring her fate within the compass of human sympathy and the poet's grasp. A name like Wragg was outside the pale. Romance was no longer bringing up the nine-fifteen.

CHAPTER II

Prose or Poetry?

IT IS arguable that the novelists rather than the poets of the nineteenth century are the real beneficiaries of the great Romantic endowment. Certainly the novel, and not the long poem, was to become the dominant literary form of the century, and the novel went on to success in a field in which poetry virtually ceased to compete—the relationship between the individual imagination and the problems and complications of society. Those who deplore the plight of contemporary poetry often ignore the fact that many of the former functions of the poet have been taken over by the novelist: the change is simply one of form.

Nor would Coleridge and Wordsworth, who always refused to make any qualitative distinction between prose and poetry, have been disconcerted by this change, one imagines. The technical requirements made verse more exacting, that was all, and the forms and technique of verse were not equal to the immense expansion of the imagination into regions which it would take prose fiction to settle and colonise. If their Romantic responsibilities were a source of difficulty and inhibition to many Victorian poets, they were to novelists like George Eliot a challenge and a joy. And the mechanism of the novel gave ample scope for dealing with them. But in verse the Romantics developed no new form; they drew heavily on the eighteenth century and on Milton, whose diction was itself the stock eighteenth-century poetic language, and they revived ballad metres and Elizabethan blank verse. Although in the sphere of the mind the movement was a revolution, in the sphere of form it was decidedly a revival. No new device was ready to the poet's hand like the decasyllabic line which had lent itself to the creative upsurge of the Renaissance and developed with it. *The Ancient Mariner* is a remarkable example of this discrepancy between form and vision. Professor Wilson Knight has not extravagantly compared it with Dante's *Purgatorio*, but its form is that of a medieval ballad, complete with Chattertonian spellings and inversions, and this has for many years obscured the fullness and significance of the poem's content and prevented them from becoming explicit in the reader's mind.

And where his blank verse is concerned Wordsworth cannot be said to have a *style* of his own, in the fullest sense, at all. As C. S. Lewis has pointed out, the mode of the long, thoughtful, and discursive poem, like Cowper's *Task* or Akenside's *Pleasures of the Imagination*, achieves its final impressiveness in the *Prelude* and *Excursion*:* in form these come at the end of a tradition, not at the beginning of one. Their detailed style moves between the 'divine chit-chat of Cowper', as Coleridge, himself a sedulous follower of Cowper's manner, so affectionately called it; the Miltonic richness of famous passages in the *Prelude*; and, less noticeable but equally pervasive, a startling resemblance to Shakespeare.

> *Oh sir, the good die first,*
> *And those whose hearts are dry as summer dust*
> *Burn to the socket—*

* On Addison. (*Essays on the 16th Century Presented to Professor Nichol-Smith*. Oxford 1945).

Wordsworth tends to fall back on other styles, and this happens—as we should expect—much more often in the *Excursion* than in the *Prelude*. The lucidity of the great passages does not come home to us in terms of style: we hardly think of them as involved in a poetic medium.

This high Romantic 'absence', as Mallarmé might have termed it, this availing yourself of any old style up to the point at which style is no longer needed, could only be a source of embarrassment to a natural stylist like Keats. I suspect that his mingled admiration and animosity for Wordsworth may have been partly caused by it. He too, in the long poem *Hyperion* and the play *Otho the Great*, is dogged by Milton and Shakespeare—much more notoriously so in fact than is Wordsworth—but in his case the debt is not a convenience but an oppression.

> *This Prince was gulled and cheated,*
> *But from the ashes of disgrace he rose*
> *More than a fiery Phoenix—and did burn*
> *His ignominy up in purging fires.*

This speech from *Otho the Great* virtually *is* Shakespeare while Wordsworth in the preceding quotation is only making use of Shakespeare; but so deep and involuntary a grasp of his model makes it all the harder for Keats to achieve that 'stylelessness', if one may call it so, which the universality claimed for the long Romantic poem seemed to entail. Indeed, if the Romantic can avail himself of any handy style or tradition in order to reach the point where an impersonal sublimity breaks in, there seems no reason why he should concern himself with form at all. Why even write in verse? And this brings us back to where we started—the Romantic refusal to distinguish between verse and prose, or rather (we must assume) between poetry and prose, for as

T. S. Eliot once observed, 'the distinction between verse and prose is clear, but that between poetry and prose much more obscure'.

Coleridge's distinction—'prose is words in the best order, poetry the best words in the best order'—though suggestive, hardly carries the matter much further. In a famous letter to Sotheby he calls 'poetical prose' 'a very vile olio', and the prose poem, *The Wanderings of Cain*, which he and Wordsworth once embarked on together, was soon given up: its Gothic and biblical overtones are much less easily made use of than the Miltonic and Shakespearean tradition in the authors' verse. Yet in some respects the prose-poem might have suited Wordsworth better for describing certain of the incidents in *Lyrical Ballads* than did the strong simple rhythms which he in fact selected. His celebrated absurdities are often striking details and observations that are only rendered ludicrous by the thump and chime of metre.

> *I've measured it from side to side,*
> *'Tis three feet long and two feet wide.*

As a telling detail in a prose narrative—'the pond in which she drowned her child was no more than three foot by two' —this would be far from absurd. As it is, there is a gap between form and sentiment which arises from the Romantic indifference to form, an indifference which often becomes uneasiness; poetry was a spirit that could theoretically be liberated through almost any medium, but in practice the media often proved unsatisfactory. Wordsworth, as Coleridge showed in his criticism of the Lyrical Ballads, had merely exchanged one set of forms for another; and though he had banished 'gawdy and inane phraseology' he was really no nearer to the ideal of poetic simplicity and purity: as we have seen in the example above, the 'inanity' of metre prevents the simplicity and force from emerging fully. 'I find', Coleridge, more clear-sighted, wrote to Wordsworth, '*I* cannot attain this innocent nakedness, except by *assumption*. I resemble the Duchess of Kingston, who masqueraded in the character of "Eve before the Fall", in flesh-coloured silk.'

'Except by *assumption*'—with characteristic humour and self-depreciation Coleridge is indicating this important aspect of the Romantic predicament: what artificial steps are best taken to assume the effect of 'innocent nakedness', of the Romantic 'absence' as we have called it? How does one write a 'Poem which affects not to be poetry', to borrow the discarded sub-title of one of Coleridge's own effusions? Clearly the logical answer is to write it in prose. And the legatees of the great Romantics, less scrupulous and en-quiring than they, in fact apply this remorselessly simple solution. A 'conversational' poem becomes still more like a conversation if it is written in prose; it is the same with narrative, or with philosophy. And though you may claim that this prose is still 'poetry', if it is good enough, that does not make the neglected verse form any less of a Cinderella. 'Lord Bacon was a poet', declares Shelley, 'Plato was a poet'. His choice of examples is significant—two philosophers who are famous for their hostile or contemptuous attitude to-wards poetry. Yet they were involuntary poets; they were actually doing what they patronised or condemned. A theory of primitivism is touched on here—Shelley seems to be claiming for later writers what he claimed for the infancy of society, 'when language itself is poetry', and the same idea clearly enters into Wordsworth's interest in the childish and the primitive. But more crucially, Shelley's line of argument seems to be: 'you only depreciate poetry because you don't realise that it is the motion and the spirit that impels science, philosophy, belles-lettres, and everything else. Depreciate verse if you like—that is just an artificial form which is sometimes used for poetry.'

This argument defeats its own purpose: instead of helping to universalise the idea of poetry it only tends to provincialise the idea of verse. Just as bad money drives out good, so prose will drive out verse, since those who use prose will do so all the more readily now that Romantic theory assures them that they can do so 'poetically'. The form of verse will now seem more specialised and artificial, less readily to be turned to by the average writer. Scott turns from verse to prose; George Eliot, who—had she lived fifty years earlier—would certainly have written in verse, is a novelist first and a versifier a long way second. The Romantic emancipation of poetry, freeing it from forms and artificialities, paradoxically ensures that verse will seem more artificial in contrast with the triumph of poetry in prose—a triumph certainly not foreseen by Sir Philip Sidney when, long before the Romantics, he first waived the distinction between the two forms.

From our point of view, exploring—as we shall try to do —the present-day position of Romanticism in verse, the triumph of prose has important consequences. One can hardly emphasise enough how little the early Romantic theories deserve such epithets as dreamy, exotic, eccentric, private, escapist, devitalised—all the adjectives which have come by association to cling to the word Romantic—nor how much they require, on the contrary, such terms as practical, sensible, unifying, all-embracing, morally aware, and so on. But as the nineteenth century goes on, it is prose that qualifies more and more for these latter attributes of the liberated imagination, and verse for the former. The old Baconian dichotomy about poetry as the mind's pleasant relaxation when exhausted by the tussle with reason and truth, has cropped up again in a different form. Though the Imagination has been promoted, verse can now become the scapegoat and repository for all mental irresponsibility and indiscipline. Verse, epitomised by such a poem as *Kubla Khan*, acquires the specialised function of dealing with and catering for the 'streamy' and 'moody' side of the mind. 'Tears, idle tears, I know not what they mean'. Coleridge, who himself regarded *Kubla Khan* as a mere curiosity, would certainly have tried to explain what they *did* mean, either in prose or in verse. But Tennyson, writing in verse—and verse moreover that is a song inside a poetical 'Medley' and so at two removes—does not and need not explain. The Romantic indifference to form ensures that verse, which has always tended to be considered irrational anyway, will now become the accepted receptacle for irrationality. As Poe, only a very few years after Wordsworth and Coleridge, finally put the matter: 'All that which is so indispensable in song is precisely all that with which [Truth] has nothing to do'.

The very word 'song' here illustrates the narrowing and defensive process which has occurred: verse has been intensified into 'song' in order to distinguish it still more from the world of prose and fact. Already in the background are phrases like Pater's 'all art aspires to the condition of music', and Croce's definition of art as 'lyrical intuition'. This is our third Romantic polarity: at one extreme we have poetry as all-inclusive, and capable 'of bringing the whole soul of man into activity'; at the other extreme, poetry—('verse' or 'song' that is)—as a fascinating secretion of the mind, yet all but meaningless in terms of the mind's other activities and co-ordinates. Somewhere between these two, 'poetry as prose', that unsettling Romantic hypothesis, has lifted its head.

Hardy is a poet of the one extreme, Housman of the second; nor is it accidental that there is so much continuity between Hardy as novelist and as lyric and dramatic poet, and so little between Housman as a poet and as a professor and editor. As Housman says quite frankly in *The Name and Nature of Poetry*, the realities of the moral world have no connection with the excitements of the poetic one, and he implies that they can hardly coexist with each other. Auden, an admirer of Housman, and also (as I shall hope to show) a poet of this type, is equally frank about the *lightness* of poetry: what was for Housman unattached mystery has become for him unattached frivolity; and it seems to me that Auden has been misread, and in consequence wrongly praised or blamed, due to a misunderstanding of his romantic attitude and origins. For him, prose, and in particular prose fiction, is the moral and responsible form. As he writes in one of the *Letters to Lord Byron:*

> *I don't know whether*
> *You will agree, but novel writing is*
> *A higher art than poetry altogether*
> *In my opinion, and success implies*
> *Both finer character and faculties.*

Byron, one imagines, might well have agreed if he had bothered about the question at all. His mind—his 'uninteresting' mind as T. S. Eliot for some reason calls it—was that of a novelist, but he enjoyed the opportunities for brilliance and ingenuity which verse presented—

> *a form that's large enough to swim in*
> *And talk on any subject that I choose.*

Apart from trouncing the clergyman Bowles for his too literal reverence for 'Nature', Byron took little interest in

the theoretical problems that inspired and bedevilled his contemporaries; but he was the only one of them to employ a
new verse technique that was unmistakably his own. Verse
was for him, as it has been for Auden, a craft to be practised
without much painful and curious regard for the metaphysical status and function of poetry.

CHAPTER III

Romance or Reality?

HALFWAY THROUGH the eighteenth century the novel had already begun to explore the world of Romance. Following *The Castle of Otranto*, published by Horace Walpole in 1764, and Leland's *Longsword* in 1762, came a stream of fiction, dealing with every aspect of the Gothic and the marvellous in a medieval or Oriental context. Poetry at this time was already exploring the world of external nature, and—particularly in the case of Crabbe and Cowper—with ever-increasing delicacy and detail. Indeed, as fiction became more fantastic, poetry tended to become more exact, and to fix its eye more and more closely on the object. This fondness for vivid, all but gratuitous detail, is notable in Coleridge.

> *. . . by yonder throstle wooed*
> *That pipes within the larch tree, not unseen,*
> *(The larch which pushes out in tassels green*
> *Its bundled leafits)—*

The sacrifice of conventional euphony to accuracy of description—especially description of mass and texture—is common in Coleridge and Keats, both of whom have a passion for the feel of detail that often over-rode decorum and would never have been ventured on by their precursors. The Romantic 'language of seeing' had to be learnt by their

24

readers, and Byron may not have been so perverse as it now appears when he protested that Coleridge's description of the evening sky 'with its peculiar tint of Yellow Green' could not have been observed in nature. But gratuitous as Coleridge's detail may sometimes seem, it reflects his constant preoccupation with the modes of perception—into both nature and the mind—and with that ordering and synthesising of visual experience which Kant had postulated as the Imagination's main function. Always on the fringes of metaphysics, Romantic poetry was in danger of becoming a purely contemplative and exploratory power which might penetrate the individual mind with the same acuteness as it penetrated external objects, but which had none the less lost the art of representing dramatically the conflicts between, say, man as an individual and as a social being, or between his illusions about his environment and the reality about it.

In Shelley's poetry, for example, conflict is seen entirely in vague mythological terms, with the poet moreover as so earnest a partisan of his own ideals that no alternatives to them seem actual. Critics have observed the absence of conflict in Keats's *Hyperion*: the two dynasties of Gods are not brought into any antagonism which would lend epic vigour and interest to the poem. Other critics—and they are no doubt right—have hastened to point out that Keats was not interested in any such antagonism but in an exploration, perhaps of something like the nature of immortality and how it is gained. At all events the poem, like the *Prelude*, is exploratory; sensitive and tentacular, the poet's mind is reaching out into the mystery of itself and its surroundings, and the process cannot but be an exceedingly undramatic one. The essence of drama is clash, irreconcilability, the gulf between God and Satan, or the Greeks and the Trojans; the essence of poetry, as the four great Romantics wrote it, is synthetic and healing, tending always towards harmony and similarity, not division and difference. And they believed that in so writing they were representing the nature of Reality.

Romantic fiction, on the other hand, was under no obligation to attempt this. Fantasy, as we have said, was here the order of the day, and where poetry was painstaking and exploratory, the novel was fanciful and irresponsible. Monks, skeletons, and black veils; enormous helmets hurled into castle courtyards; the endless adventures of the illegitimate children of Mary Queen of Scots—anything and everything went that could be suggested by the humble associative powers of Romantic Fancy; and the status of the novel was in consequence low. How low we can gather from Jane Austen's humorous account in *Northanger Abbey*, written in 1798; but it is this and Jane Austen's other novels, and Scott's *Waverley*, published in 1814, which first showed how the immense fictional resources of Romance could best be used.

The novel, unlike poetry, had no self-appointed metaphysical responsibility; it was popular; and it had a tradition of realism that went back to the theatre—Fielding had been a dramatist before he began to write fiction. In the eighteenth century, novels of the picaresque or sentimental kind, with a background close to human affairs and a straightforward moral viewpoint, overlapped for many years with Gothic Romances on the one hand and works of didactic and militant Romanticism, like *La Nouvelle Heloïse* and *The Sorrows of Werther*, on the other. Between these three kinds there was little fusion, and the point of view represented by each was essentially single-minded. None showed any indecision about what constituted the true or the false, the fantastic or the actual, but each located these things in different places; and each demanded of their readers a simple kind of assent, enthusiasm, or suspension of disbelief: the reader agreed with Fielding, was enthralled by Monk Lewis, and blew out his brains or eloped after reading Goethe or Rousseau—but each reaction was on its own separate plane. It was the achievement of Scott and Jane Austen to bring these planes of fantasy and reality into one book, one vision of life, and to show how they conflicted with each other; the two authors initiated that complex of appearance and reality which has constituted the *mise en scène* and battle-ground of the mature novel ever since.

In speaking of appearance and reality I am not implying that novelists since Jane Austen and Scott have been engaged with a philosophical question that has exercised philosophers from Plato to F. H. Bradley. From the novelist's point of view, he himself is the sole arbiter of what constitutes both: he can decide, or he can deliberately refrain from deciding, where reality in the world of his novel lies, and he can show how it conflicts with the subjective world of make-believe which his characters embody or explore. Jane Austen, like Cervantes, satirises Romantic absurdity, but where Cervantes and the picaresque writers who followed him are concerned only with story-telling in the old two-dimensional sense, she presents us with a fictional complex in which illusion enriches the real world and is closely related to it. That world is 'the midland counties of England' where human nature shows 'a general though unequal mixture of good and bad', and it is ironically contrasted with the 'pine forests and vices' of Southern Europe. 'The visions of romance were over. Catherine was completely awakened.' After her fantastic notions of what is going on in the Tilney household, her return to reality is comparable, on the satirical plane, with the more serious disillusionment of Marianne Dashwood and Emma Woodhouse. All three novels take their rise from the contrast between the nature of society (as Jane Austen ultimately sees it) and the heroine's illusions or mistakes about it. Moreover illusion and reality enrich one another in a positive way: though General Tilney is not a Gothic ogre he is in fact a highly disagreeable man, as full of illusions about Catherine as she is about him. So illusion is a more complicated process than might appear, and one illusion—however grotesque—may serve to show the nature of another and subtler one. With the help of Gothic Romance Jane Austen is enabled to examine more deeply the nature of a humdrum social situation: she makes Romance throw a searching light on the nature of reality.

It is difficult for us now to understand the enormous enthusiasm which greeted the appearance of *Waverley*. Though its permanent place among the world's novels may not be very high, it is a far better and less simple book than is usually supposed, not perhaps, what Virginia Woolf called *Middlemarch*—'one of the few English novels written for grown-up people'—but certainly indicating how such novels might subsequently be written. Alone of the Romantics, Scott was able to make effective use of the Shakespearean tradition, and his popularity is closely connected with the steady growth of Shakespeare's reputation throughout the eighteenth century. We have seen how Romantic poetry imitated Shakespeare's style, but neither poetry nor the drama was able to profit from the world of his plays. Fiction did so; the conflict between two worlds, two ideals, which is the basis of so many—and of the histories in particular—is profoundly understood by Scott and adapted to his own purposes, unconsciously perhaps, but with results of the highest importance. Shakespeare does not judge between his two worlds; he does not 'prefer' Richard II to Bolingbroke, or Hotspur to Prince Hal, and this dramatic neutrality

is introduced by Scott into the fictional world; he is not on
the romantic side of the Pretender or on the prosaic side of
King George: he is content to show them in conflict, as he
presents the Covenanters and the Royalists in *Old Mortality*,
or the English and Scottish ways of life in *The Two Drovers*;
and he accords either side the kind of intuitive sympathy
which Keats, in relation to Shakespeare, had called Negative
Capability. Indeed, Keats's perception of the Shakespearean
approach fits Scott better than any of the other Romantics,
including—at least on the human and dramatic level—Keats
himself.

In contrast with such ill-fated young Romantics as
Goethe's Werther and Büchner's Lenz, Waverley may be
said to be the first *successful* Romantic hero, the first who is
robust enough and has sufficient powers of self-acclimatisa-
tion to achieve the feat which Catherine Morland—due to
the limitations of her age and sex, and her creator's satiric
purpose—had scarcely attempted. Waverley eats his cake
and has it; he enjoys the best of both worlds like Shakespeare's Prince Hal, although he is a much more attractive
character. After his successful flirtation with the world of
Romance and illusion he returns to the humdrum Hano-
verian world. He fights in the Pretender's army, but he
comes back safely to his English estate; he falls in love with
the Romantic Flora MacIvor, but he marries the domesti-
cated Rose Bradwardine. The book has its tragedy—Fergus
MacIvor, like Hotspur, pays with his life the penalty of
living too completely in the world of illusion. Nor is it
without humour: Scott knew well that the Laird of Abbots-
ford could point out exactly where sensibility should leave
off and sense begin. Yet Scott's humour is not satiric—the
romantic afflatus of the tale only gains from it, and the new
fictional formula is as far from Don Quixote on the one

hand as it is from Werther and the Nouvelle Heloïsc on the other. Scott's world has a total sanity in which Romance and Reality both have their place and are finally reconciled.

This English compromise does not occur in France, where the seminal power of Scott's genius and the possibilities of development his rich formula offered were quickly appreciated. Transposed into such French terms as the antithesis between Romantic and Bourgeois, his two worlds are exhaustively explored by Balzac and Flaubert. Lucien de Rubempré in *Les Illusions Perdues* is a Waverley who goes to Paris instead of to the Highlands, and whose final end corresponds with the nature of the life he finds there. Balzac moves with equal facility between the high Romanticism of *Seraphita* and *La Recherche de L'Absolu*, and the extreme realism of *La Rabouilleuse* and *Le Père Goriot*: we may prefer the latter, but there is no doubt that he is equally at home in both worlds, and both are complementary in his picture of the human comedy.

In *Madame Bovary*, Flaubert applies the Romantic formula in, so to speak, its most classic form. The mean actuality of provincial life is contrasted with the romantic desires of Emma Bovary, who, like the more fortunate Emma Woodhouse, is in a state of illusion, but one from which her creator never allows her to recover. Like Scott, Flaubert never judges the two worlds, but he insists, perhaps rather too rigorously, that a conflict between them can only end in disaster. In France the Romantic dualism has always taken an extreme form, and the transcendental few—Baudelaire's dandys, Rimbaud's seers, Sartre's *engagés*, and other *authentiques* of various denominations—have always sharply excluded themselves from the bourgeois and the *tièdes*. Balzac, perhaps alone of nineteenth-century French authors, appreciated to the full the discovery made by Scott, and which indeed seems peculiarly likely to have been made in England, that the romantic and the humdrum world were not irreconcilable but could be made to enhance one another. The English capacity to resolve the dualism may make for less impressive ideologies than the French, but it perhaps also makes for a fuller and richer treatment of the writer's material. James Joyce's story *The Dead* is an outstanding example. His sympathy with both the bourgeois and the romantic ideal is shown in his description of a dead man's passion for a happily married wife, set against the background of a superbly detailed bourgeois "soirée" which leads both husband and wife back to a vision of the past event.

What has all this to do with later romantic poetry? As we have said, the poetry of the four great Romantics is groping and exploratory; it is never dramatic, in the sense that it is never content to watch human beings and their affairs in action, but is always asking Why? What is the enigma of the leech-gatherer, the old soldier? Why do men—and Man in general—excite the imagination as they do? What is the mystery behind it all? Fiction and the drama, on the other hand, tend to accept their materials, and to present them to their audience as something in *action*, rather than as something waiting to be explored. The spectator or reader is passive, watching a conflict in which he is not called upon to engage himself, and enjoying character—like that of Falstaff or Goriot or Balfour of Burley—simply for what it is, whereas in early Romantic poetry the probing process of the poet's imagination depends for its success upon the full co-operation of the reader in the same voyage of discovery. The literature of question and exploration demands the reader's attention much more fully than the literature of action and acceptance. Ideally, of course, the two are not separated but coexist on different levels: the reader of Shakespeare is first passively engaged by action and personality in conflict, and is then drawn—if he is capable and so desires—into the underlying exploratory movement of the poet's mind. As Coleridge says: 'You feel him (Shakespeare) to be a poet, inasmuch as for a time he has made you one.' But in early Romantic poetry (by which term I refer principally to the four great Romantics) it is, so to speak, exploration all the way: our participation is always required; we are never allowed to repose in the enjoyment of a dramatic *fait accompli*. In romantic fiction, as with Scott for example, or Joyce, or Flaubert, precisely the opposite is true. We do not feel ourselves to be, in some sense, a necessary extension of the writer's mind: he is a Deus Absconditus towards the quality of whose mind we remain largely indifferent.

Now, for reasons which were discussed earlier, fiction grew to be the dominant form in the nineteenth century, and soon began to inherit the great self-imposed responsibilities of the early Romantics. But there was another side to the question. Engrossed in exploration, poetry surrendered the province of human drama and conflict almost wholly to the new form. And fiction, even as it grew more respectable, retained none the less the traditions of a form to which the concept of belief as it is given in the poet's world—the assent or dissent of the reader's whole personality—was hardly relevant. There is as it were a timelag between the *de facto* ascendancy of fiction and its *de jure* recognition as a form as 'serious' as poetry; and meanwhile there had become established as a criterion of the novel's success the temporary assent the reader gave to the fictional world involved. 'Enjoy a good action, a good story, and don't bother about anything else. Practise a controlled yielding to the mood and values of the piece, whether it is set in a boarding-house dining-room or the cave of a Highland bandit: it is well understood by both author and reader that his world is imaginary, and to be enjoyed for its own sake.' Some such critical verdict might have been made on the novel's function if it had been worth anyone's while to make it. As it was, the novel helped to set up the characteristic late romantic tendency to distinguish between what we enjoy and what we value, a distinction that could often lead, as we saw in the case of Poe and Housman, to the separation of art from all moral values. The Victorian critic Dallas puts the issue squarely, if defensively, when he says: 'The deliberate selection of a lower form of pleasure does not interfere with our estimate of the higher.'★

When poetry began again to employ dramatic and fictional methods, as in the Dramatic Monologue so popular with Browning and later nineteenth-century poets, and in the Mask technique of Yeats, it tended to incur as well the fictional criterion of response. From the dramatic form in which most of his poetry is cast, Browning emerges as a man, like Balzac, obsessed with the worthwhileness of action and vigour for its own sake.

Noon strikes—, here sweeps the procession! Our Lady borne
smiling and smart
With a pink gauze gown all spangles, and seven swords stuck
in her heart!

The picture is ours. An early Romantic poet like Wordsworth would have mingled his description, had he given it, with comments on church ceremonial and the arguments for Rome, but mingled is the wrong word, for in Wordsworth's whole approach, vision, comment, exploration, are

★ Dallas, *The Gay Science.*

33

indivisible. Browning, writing under fictional licence and in the person of an 'Italian gentleman of quality', can indulge his interest in human colour and vitality without further responsibility. When he feels it necessary to include a moral, or to make the poem appear a discovery about the nature of life—as in *The Statue and the Bust*, for instance—the result is not so satisfactory. His strength, like Scott's, or that of any good story-teller, is of a difficult kind to define: it cannot be conveyed in the form of ideas or a philosophy—it is essentially on the spot, in the impact of each poem on the reader. Nor is the 'good strong story' type of poem, the dramatic monologue, confined at this date to Browning. If we compare Tennyson's *Maud* and *Rizpah* and Hardy's *A Tramp-Woman's Tragedy*, with *Peter Bell*, or *Christabel*, the difference between poetry as dramatic fiction and as imaginative exploration is clear enough. Nor is it necessarily to the disadvantage of the former: the two kinds are complementary and require to be judged by different standards. It would be quite possible to see the transition from one to the other as a decline from exploration to sensation, a coarsening of the Romantic fibre. If we were intent on measuring the decline of Romanticism, this would certainly be a critical point as legitimate as T. S. Eliot's discovery of the 'dissociation of sensibility' that overtook English poetry at the end of the seventeenth century. Critics are never wanting who see all change in the world of poetry as impoverishment. But as we have pointed out, whatever else its shortcomings, by allying itself with fictional methods the romantic poetry of the latter half of the nineteenth century, and beyond, succeeded in supplying precisely the elements that had been lacking to the poets of the Romantic Revival.

Yeats, who as a young man defined truth to his father as 'dramatic utterance raised to the highest pitch of passion', takes naturally to the tradition of dramatic monologue and produces his own personal variation of it in the doctrine of the Mask, the dramatic attitudes that the author himself—in his own person—may strike in turn, in order to increase the limits of his experience and exhibit it more effectively in action. The resemblance to drama and fiction is clear: reality may emerge if contrary appearances, ideas, or 'dreams' are violently confronted with each other—if it does not, well, the virtue of the poem lies in the attempt. This scepticism about truth and the conviction that the 'doing' is what matters in poetry, the hunt is more important than the quarry, accompanies Yeats's whole poetic development. In a very early poem he writes

> *Of old the world on dreaming fed;*
> *Grey truth is now her painted toy.*

In a late poem, *Vacillation*, a dialogue occurs in which The Soul says

> *Seek out reality, leave things that seem,*

and The Heart replies

> *What, be a singer born and lack a theme?*

As befits the change in Yeats's style, 'Reality' and 'seeming' are bleaker and more sharply defined terms than 'dreaming' and 'grey truth', but they amount to the same thing. 'Reality' is not in moods and illusions, but moods and illusions, Yeats seems to be saying, are the subject of poetry: the dilemma can be resolved by a dramatic conflict between the two.

There is of course much more to Yeats's theory of the Mask than this, and we must reserve a discussion of its larger implications for the chapter on the poet himself. Yeats was ambitious to be a poet of the exploratory kind and to construct a metaphysical system analogous to those of the early Romantics, but it is difficult not to feel that his virtues are primarily those which I have called dramatic. And such virtues are self-sufficient. We no more think of asking if Yeats really believed in the theological complex set out in *A Vision* than we ask if Balzac (of whose novels Yeats was a great admirer) believes in the Swedenborgianism with which he mysticises the human comedy.

With W. H. Auden we find the poet's view of life as dramatic opposition extended into a whole detailed world of personal images and correspondencies. His shadowy frontier wars, the perpetual struggle which is being waged in incongruous surroundings—over tea-tables, in derelict factories and in the Golf Club bar—what an admirable setting they provide for dramatic conflict. Again, however, we may find ourselves thinking that what matters to the poetry is the conflict itself, rather than its causes or its outcome. How it is presented, in all the arresting detail of fiction, is well shown in two stanzas from a poem originally in *The Orators*, in the Collected Edition renamed with significant self-irony *Which side am I Supposed to be on?*

Now we're due to parade on the square in front of the Cathedral,
When the bishop has blessed us, to file in after the choirboys,
To stand with the wine-dark conquerors in the roped-off pews,
*   Shout ourselves hoarse:*
'They ran like hares; we have broken them up like firewood;
*   They fought against God'.*

While in a great rift in the limestone miles away
At the same hour they gather, tethering their horses beside them;

A scarecrow prophet from a boulder foresees our judgement,
   Their oppressors howling;
And the bitter psalm is caught by the gale from the rocks:
   'How long shall they flourish?'

Though it is possible to find out who *We* and *They* are,
more or less, from our knowledge of what Auden approves
and disapproves of at this period, it is difficult to feel that
this knowledge adds to our pleasure in the poem or alters
our feelings about its quality. This is tantamount to saying
that a total scrutiny of all that is in it is not a necessary step
to procuring the full enjoyment it has to offer—which in
some critical circles today would be a very damning assertion to make about a poem. We shall later be enquiring into
this matter more fully, but for the moment the point to be
noticed is how certain striking features of Auden's work fall
naturally into the tradition of the dramatic monologue, the
Mask, and the fictional approach. We have already noticed
his regard for the novelist's art, and the last quotation shows
obvious affinities of local colour with Scott's novels (particularly *Old Mortality*), or with Stevenson. It may seem art-
less to assert so homely an analogue in the case of a poet as
intellectually well-connected and as sensitive to the fashions
of modern thought as Auden has always shown himself to
be, but it is precisely such simple forbears—rather than
Groddeck or Malinowski—whose obscure strength can be
felt in him. He owes more to Scott and Hardy than to
Kierkegaard, and the tradition in which his writing is unconsciously founded is not an intellectual one.

Just as Yeats retains a very similar attitude to poetry
throughout the changes in his style, so Auden still uses this
fictional technique, telling a tale with all the impersonal
gusto of the Victorians. 'Deftly, Admiral, cast your fly',

he exhorts a retired sailor—

> *Till the wise old trout mistake and die;*
> *Salt are the deeps that cover*
> *The glittering fleets you led*
> *White is your head.*

> *Read on, ambassador, engrossed*
> *In your favourite Stendhal;*
> *The outer provinces are lost,*
> *Unshaven horsemen swill*
> *The great wines of the Chateaux*
> *Where you danced long ago.*

> *Do not turn, do not lift, your eyes*
> *Toward the still pair standing*
> *On the bridge between your properties,*
> *Indifferent to your minding:*
> *In its glory, in its power,*
> *This is their hour.*

> *Nothing your strength, your skill, could do*
> *Can alter their embrace*
> *Or dispersuade the Furies who*
> *At the appointed place*
> *With claw and dreadful brow*
> *Wait for them now.*

Although this little poem is entitled *Song*, it puts us as vividly 'in the picture' as if it were the synopsis of some long novel or legendary play-cycle. There are the two fathers with their backgrounds of personal and national defeat, conveyed with Auden's usual brilliance of sinister suggestion; the psychological pointers—in the word *deftly* and the reference to Stendhal—that they are men of real accomplishment whom a calamitous period of history (which may still be going on) proved too much for; the suggestion, too, that where the impersonal forces of history are concerned the personal skills are as helpless as they are against the forces of love which we meet in the next stanza. In this Romeo and Juliet or St Agnes' Eve situation (admiral and ambassador appear now as hostile neighbours in a background of social comedy), their children will discover, perhaps more effectively than they, the power and the glory pictured retrospectively in the first two stanzas, but they are also fated to undergo some corresponding estrangement or defeat. This prophecy completes the regular arch of the poem in the last stanza—the concrete vigour of *claw and dreadful brow* balancing that of *unshaven horsemen swill*. Auden is fond of the note of foreboding or determinism—

> *Every farthing of the cost,*
> *All the dreaded cards foretell,*
> *Shall be paid . . .*

—perhaps because it is so structurally effective and spans the lyric as effectively as the tragedy. As Chekhov said, the best short stories could also be long stories, and the compression in these twenty-four lines could be indefinitely expanded— an expansion that takes place in the reader's mind.

Browning (out of many poems one might instance *Confessions*), and Hardy in a poem like *The Frozen Greenhouse*, had much to do with the development of what might be called the sung short story; and Auden is its pre-eminent exponent today. It gives him a stylised but extraordinarily comprehensive grasp on the multiplicity of human affairs— political and social, comic and tragic—in which the detail of prose is combined with the feeling traditional to verse or ballad. Poetry is here abreast of the everyday life which had been rejected so completely by the Symbolists and others at an earlier period; and we must now turn back to see how this rejection took place.

CHAPTER IV

The World or the Mind?

As we have seen, the sensitive point in the structure of early Romantic theory is the relationship between the poet's mind and the world which it contemplates: at this point his consciousness recoils again and again on itself. Is the real world the domain of the poet's imagination, in which, like a king, it has its duties and responsibilities, or is the poet concerned only with a world perceived and created by his own mind? In so far as the world is dead, stupid, intractable, a gross materialistic presence, may the poet ignore it—or must he attempt to make all come to life under the power of the imagination?

Conscience inclined the English poets to the latter duty, but not so in France. Less susceptible to German metaphysics, and with Montaigne rather than Hamlet in their blood, the French poets preserved a traditional realism. Wordsworth and Coleridge were hardly heard of, and Baudelaire and de Nerval would have been genuinely surprised to learn that it was their function as poets to expound and justify the ways of the imagination to men. They saw themselves as isolated, disinherited like the *El Desdichado* of de Nerval's poem, proud and alien figures in a materialist society in which they had no place. They welcomed *Childe Harold* but not *The Friend*: the evangelical urge and the civic sense have never been strong in French poetry. The difference is plain in their treatment of the stock Romantic images. For Coleridge the albatross is an image of the sacredness of life; its death makes a division in the universal order which can only be healed by the suffering of the individual concerned. And it is the lost companionship of living things, whether they are the sailors—'the many men so beautiful'—or the water-snakes, which this individual feels so acutely. For him, the universe—in the words of Catherine in *Wuthering Heights*—has 'turned to a mighty stranger'. But for Baudelaire this state of affairs is what the poet expects and exults in (for Coleridge the victim was not a 'poet' but 'a man speaking to men'), and for Baudelaire it is the albatross who represents the poet and whose *ailes de géant s'empêchent de marcher* when he is caught by the sailors and forced to submit to the humiliation of an alien world—the world in which, according to Wordsworth, 'we find our happiness, or not at all'. Happiness, which, as a common human end, is important to Wordsworth, is supremely unimportant to Baudelaire. The poet expects to do without such things.

But the French did not give up the Romantic conception of the poet as a man of power. Only the 'hiding-places' of that power have changed, and they are to be searched for in a different way. The poet is no longer an unacknowledged legislator, but a magician, a *déchiffreur*, as Baudelaire calls him, of the riddles of the universe. And a magician cannot be expected to occupy himself with ordinary human affairs: the change in terminology shows a change of heart. In France, after the failure of the Revolution of 1848, which Baudelaire seems to have supported only as an act of defiance against his father-in-law, who was a general on the government side, Romanticism ceases to take much interest in political and social problems. In England, Tennyson and Arnold were doing their best to make their poetry a criticism

of Victorian life; but as the Romantic movement returned
from France in the shape of Symbolism, the poet rejected—
as Yeats put it—'the view that poetry is a criticism of life,
and became more and more convinced that it is a revelation
of a hidden life'. The poet is going underground. His claim
now is his ability to initiate the chosen into the great secret,
which, though all-embracing, is mysterious and only to be
understood by the few. As Schuré modestly puts it in *Les
Grands Initiés: La doctrine esotérique n'est pas seulement une
science, une philosophie, une morale, une religion,—elle est* la
science, la *philosophie* and so forth. Blake and Wordsworth
had symbolised mystery and power by the simplest means—
the grain of sand, the caterpillar on the leaf—universal order
can be deduced from the smallest fragments of being. By
their very commonness these symbols emphasise man's
social nature, what he shares with his fellows, 'the human
heart by which we live'. But for the magician poet the idea
of a common symbol is repellent; images that enabled the
early Romantic to see into the life of things are for the
youthful Yeats only a painful interruption of a private
intensity.

The cry of a child by the roadway, the creak of a lumbering cart,
The heavy steps of the ploughman splashing the wintry mould
Are wronging your image that blossoms a rose in the deeps of my
        heart.

Symbolist theory, it is difficult not to feel, tries to have it
both ways—while asserting the unity of experience it cuts
itself off from everything that might give sense and
weight to such a unity. And as the materials of the symbolists
grow more rarefied and the scale of their performance
diminishes, their theories grow ever more insistent and more
elaborate. The idea of imaginative synthesis is worked to

death in such extravagances as that poetry exists to evoke *le son d'une odeur, la couleur d'une note, le parfum d'une pensée,* and 'the new poetic system' that was evolved on the basis of Rimbaud's sonnet on the colours of the different vowels. Vanor, who defines these aims for the poet in *L'Art Symboliste,* announces that *un jour il dira aux hommes le mot de Dieu et le secret de la vie.* One cannot help wondering how the word of God and the secret of life is to emerge from the colour of a note and the perfume of a thought. This is magic with a vengeance. Even Mallarmé and Valéry often speak of poetry in terms of the conjuror's wand, though as we shall see, magic for them lay in the power of words themselves. The magician is single-minded—*tout au monde existe pour aboutir à un livre,* said Mallarmé; while for the celebrated Axel of Villiers de L'Isle Adam the kingdom of his own mind is quite enough: all Romantic voyages and experiences, however exotic, are for him equally banal, and—'as for living, our servants will do that for us'. The poet as hierophant and recluse has taken over entirely from the poet as explorer and philosopher.

In the course of the century the Romantic preoccupation with the relationship between the creator and his material took every possible form and carried every implication to its most explicit conclusions. Axel's disdain for the world, an attitude which the symbolists found so arresting, is already foreshadowed in Blake's rejection of 'the vegetable universe'; Valéry's fascination with the realm of pure thought and with the creative process reminds us of Coleridge at the other end of the century. Keats's remarks on Negative Capability and the poet as a 'chameleon', a being without convictions and personality of his own who momentarily assumes the colour of whatever he writes about, become highly sympathetic to a period which Pater rather equivo-

44

cally calls 'so rich and various in special apprehensions of the truth'. Ethical irresponsibility, or rather subsuming ethics and aesthetics under the same range of responses, follows naturally if Keats's casual remarks are too methodically treated; but though it led to many *fin-de-siècle* eccentricities, distrust of the aloof and solitary imagination dispensing wisdom and understanding from a fixed standpoint also led in more fruitful directions. Pater's attitudes for overcoming the dilemma remind us of those of Keats, but he employs no metaphor of entering into the life around him: his consciousness is frankly static, but he accepts its judgements wholeheartedly, however ephemeral and contradictory they may be and however incapable of erection into a system. Truth is relative, and the only truth worth having is that which appears and disappears with every instant of the alert imagination's response to its surroundings. The Paterian solution is neither a retreat into the mind nor an attempt to enter the phenomena of the external world, but a frank assertion that the mind's successive *aperçus*, its privileged moments when it is in harmony with what it perceives, and burns (in the notorious phrase) with a hard gem-like flame—these are what is worth having, and when they occur in the artist's experience they can be transmitted to, or rather picked up by, his audience—('we overheard you O Master'). The poet is not 'a man speaking to men', but a man whose consciousness is open to the public if they are interested.

Pater's general position and its relation to the rest of Romantic theory could hardly be better summed up than in this extract from the Epilogue to *The Renaissance*.

At first sight experience seems to bury us under a flood of external objects, pressing upon us with a sharp and importunate reality, calling us out of ourselves in a thousand forms of action. But when reflection begins to play upon these objects they are dissipated under its influence; the cohesive force seems suspended like some trick of magic; each object is loosed into a group of impressions—colour, odour, texture,—in the mind of the observer. And if we continue to dwell in thought on this world, not of objects in the solidity with which language invests them, but of impressions, unstable, flickering, inconsistent, which burn and are extinguished with our consciousness of them, it contracts still further:—the whole scope of observation is dwarfed into the narrow chamber of the individual mind. . . . Every one of those impressions is the impression of an individual in his isolation, each mind keeping as a solitary prisoner its own dream of a world.

'The cohesive force seems suspended like some trick of magic'—it is almost a reversal of the idea that the imagination has a unifying power over external phenomena. Pater's awareness of individual isolation is what we should expect, but he accepts it with equanimity, and even hints that recognition of it might be the basis of a new artistic process. Protected by its passive, everchanging nature, the new sensibility is excused from the duties and responsibilities which the first Romantics had held inseparable from the poet's office. There is a similarity here to Yeats's conception of the Masks: Pater's sensibility is the passive equivalent of Yeats's artificially dynamic one. But more important is the abandonment of the poetic eminence—the 'dread watchtower' has become a 'narrow chamber', and this admission leads to developments like Proust's treatment of his characters from a relative standpoint, showing them against a continually shifting background of individual judgements and points of

view; and Virginia Woolf's convention of brilliant helpless-
ness in face of the intractability of sense experience. At first
sight the latter seems a perfect example of the Paterian consciousness, at once privileged and imprisoned, doomed to
observe the perpetual drift of events without attempting to
distinguish or qualify them. But this appearance is misleading. In fact her policy is to carry the Paterian consciousness
one stage further, and to ignore completely the distinction
between the subjective observer and the objective flux which
has always fascinated and bedevilled Romantic theory.

She attempts instead—and particularly in *The Waves*, her
boldest experiment—to create a kind of communal consciousness, in which the problems of individuality are suspended. At this level there is no character in the accepted
sense and therefore no 'I and Not-I'. In *The Waves* the individuality of the six characters is brought about not by the
way in which their minds work, for all share the same kind
of mental process, but by the different sets of images and
associations in which their vision of life embodies itself, and
even these are to a large extent shared in common. Moreover the events of their lives—earning money, making love,
pulling on stockings, eating in a restaurant—mix and mingle
with the activity of their minds, their judgements and
memories. She seems to feel that there is a sense in which
everyone's response to external events is the same, and had
therefore best be rendered in the same idiom. And if this
basic fellowship in receptivity exists, then the isolation of
which Pater and the Romantics generally are so conscious
becomes much less of a problem. Not only do inside and
outside, the world and the mind, melt into each other, but
—when she succeeds—we feel the common factor in our
consciousness has been isolated and presented in imaginative
terms. To be sure, this factor has its limitations: the conven-

tional method of describing character by dwelling on its uniqueness and on individual peculiarities usually seems closer to our actual experience of other people than does Virginia Woolf's method. Usually, but not always; for although when we think of other people as the banker, the society woman, the farmer's wife, 'the greengrocer who posts his football coupon', they appear quite separated—both from each other and from ourselves—if we are introduced into the world of their perceptions the fixed barriers of personality begin to disappear: what created the barriers is the public side of these people, their jobs, their opinions, and their capacity for emotion, and it is these things to which Virginia Woolf, though she can describe them beautifully, remains indifferent and even hostile. It is no accident that her most brilliant 'character' portrait in the conventional sense —Mr Ramsay in *To the Lighthouse*—is also the *loneliest* of her characters. 'We perished, each alone', he chants as he strides along the terrace, alarming and alienating his children and guests. His position, his theories and prejudices, his pathos, his irritable rectitude, the uncomprehending violence of his love, all make him a 'character', and all exclude him— Virginia Woolf seems to be saying—from the community of perception. She distrusts the moral and emotional life— 'love and religion'—all that its early explorers had most associated with the imagination; but she trusts the mysteriously intercommunicable power of aesthetic experience. The emotions separate, but the sensations unite: that seems to be the synthesis between world and mind which she puts forward.

CHAPTER V

Romantic or Classic?

THE CLASSICAL Revival—to give it for the moment a
text-book title—which took place at the beginning of the
present century, and which can most conveniently be associated with Paul Valéry in France and with T. E. Hulme,
Ezra Pound, and T. S. Eliot in England, arose directly out
of the Romantic absorption in the nature of the creative
process. Classicism is always associated with form, with careful craftsmanship, and with an interest in techniques for their
own sake, and paradoxically it was precisely these things to
which Romantic solipsism and self-consciousness began to
tend. A preoccupation with the techniques of knowing and
imagining easily evoked its converse—a preoccupation with
the techniques of expression. But whereas for Virginia
Woolf and Pater the problems of expression and of the
writer's subject seemed one and the same, and their solution
what Baudelaire called 'that suggestive magic including the
world outside the artist and the artist himself', for the new
adherents of the Classic ideal the resources of the mind and
its particular gift of expression are seen as largely separated
from each other. For Valéry, thought is one thing, poetry is
another, and the latter is seen as a formal quirk of the
thinker's mind, indulged in rather as a mathematician might
amuse himself with chess problems. Valéry can envisage a
time, he says, when poetry will be as extinct as heraldry or

falconry. De Quincey's idea of owing power to poetry—
'that is, exercise and expansion to your latent capacity of
sympathy with the infinite, and in relation to the great moral
capacities of man'—would have no meaning for Valéry.
Thought can do these things perhaps, but not poetry. 'The
thinker', according to Valéry, 'is trying to fix or create a
notion which is power or an instrument for obtaining power,
while the modern poet tries to produce a state in the reader,
and to carry this exceptional state to the point of perfect enjoyment'. We seem to be back at the Baconian distinction
between the reality of reason and the fantasy of poetry, a
distinction which had always been implied in the Augustan
and Classical tradition, and which Peacock had stated in its
extremest form by saying that poetry was the rattle and
plaything of society.

The tentative and exploratory note so often found in
Romantic poetry is thus quite absent in Valéry. The poet's
attitude has crystallised before he begins to write; the ground
swell of half-conscious yearnings and dilemmas is replaced
by the confidence of calm and poise. *L'amertume est douce,
et l'esprit clair.* Valéry claims that he wrote *Le Cimetière
Marin* in order to demonstrate a particular stanza form, and
the chief claim he makes for his poetry is that it shows how
adequate the Alexandrine and other traditional verse forms
still are, and discredits *vers libre*. He protests that he does not
care much about poetry, even though—like the differential
calculus—its exercise is so difficult. *Je n'y crois pas*, he says,
and the exclamation may remind us of Keats's remark in a
letter: 'I have no trust whatever in poetry—I only wonder
why people read so much of it'. Keats's tone, half sad, half
jocular, already carries a hint of what is for Valéry deliberate
and calculated policy—the refusal to revere the mystery as
critics like Schuré and Vanor did, the refusal to regard poetry

in the portentous high Romantic fashion. Valéry enjoys de-
bunking 'isms', even the symbolism mystique of Mallarmé
which had influenced him so much as a young man. 'Enthusiasm', he says in a famous phrase, 'is not the artist's state
of mind'. He substitutes for the Romantic conceptions of
the poet as mystic, moralist, or magician, a conception of the
poet as a kind of specialised intellectual juggler.

But 'intellectual' is the key word: although Valéry does
not revere the function of poetry he dislikes the idea of it
being separate from any other form of intellectual activity.
'I could not bear', he says in *Memoires d'un Poème*, 'that the
poetic state should be set in opposition to the full and sus-
tained activity of the intellect.' Coleridge might have made
the same comment. But Coleridge would not have viewed
the intellect as Valéry's Monsieur Teste, with his lucid,
mirror-like awareness of his own mental processes, does so.
Though the unveiling of the unconscious mental processes
fascinated Coleridge, he never ceased to respect the fact that
their power proceeded from their fundamental obscurity,
that they must be judged by the weight of their impact on
the conscious mind, not by the extent to which they could
be understood and 'mirrored' by that mind. For Valéry,
however, mystery (in the traditional and to him doubtless
rather absurd sense in which the word is used in connection
with poetry and words) resides in being precise, and the
greater the precision that words can be made to obtain, the
more 'mysterious' the discerning intellect will find them
to be.

By T. E. Hulme in England, the concept of precision, of
hardness and dryness in poetry, was taken up as an anti-
romantic battlecry. But whereas Valéry had wisely refrained,
in employing the concept, from distinguishing between the
conventional poetic categories of form and content, or

thought and expression, Hulme and the other Imagist writers appear to consider classical precision as an affair of expression pure and simple. For Valéry the ideal of language was not the old classical ideal of 'what oft was thought but ne'er so well expressed', but words so well expressed that they could not possibly have been thought before—a creation of language that is necessarily also a creation of thought. The theory underlying this approach is an important one which has had great influence on contemporary criticism, and we must return to it later; but it is certainly not an idea which engaged the attention of Hulme and the Imagists, who maintained that 'subject doesn't matter', and whose criterion was: 'Did the poet have an actually realised visual object before him in which he delighted? It doesn't matter if it were a lady's shoe or the starry heavens'.* Hulme goes so far as to revive the old categories of Fancy and Imagination, and to maintain that Fancy, by which he seems to mean a certain zestful accuracy of language—he gives Herrick's *tempestuous petticoat* as an example—is a superior function, and one which is urgently needed after the prolonged supremacy of the Romantic Imagination.

In practice, Hulme's theories had the curious effect of shrinking the field of poetry to a grotesquely Lilliputian size. Poems themselves became minute. Hulme's Complete Poetical Works—as he ironically called them—consist of five poems of which the longest is only nine lines. Ezra Pound's notorious little poem

> *Spring*
> *Too long*
> *Gongula*

is the *reductio ad absurdum* of this tendency in Imagism, and

* *Speculations*, p. 137.

substitutes a telegraphic obscurity for the dryness and hardness demanded by Hulme. F. S. Flint was eager to introduce the stiff little forms of the Japanese *Tanka* and *Haikai*, and H. D., the American Imagist, was writing poems with what Robert Graves has called 'a false classical atmosphere', in which mention of crocuses or dryads apparently ensured the form a sufficiently unromantic flavour. For many of the Imagists the antithesis between classic and romantic was of a singularly naive and literal kind, and this naiveté appears in the four tenets of the Imagist movement. (1) Direct treatment of the *thing*, whether objective or subjective. (2) Use no word that does not contribute to the presentation. (3) Compose in sequence of the musical phrase, not in sequence of the metronome. (4) Conform to the Doctrine of the Image. The precise nature of this doctrine was not vouchsafed to the general public on the grounds that they would not understand it. After so much dryness and hardness this sudden intrusion of the occult reminds us that Imagism had not put the Romanticism of the nineteenth century quite behind it.

Even more important than his insistence on the virtues of classical expression was Hulme's exposition of what was held to be the classical metaphysics. 'The view which regards man as a well, a reservoir full of possibilities, I call the romantic; the one which regards him as a very finite and fixed creature I call the classical.'* And since man is a finite creature his poems must also be finite; there must be an end to these aspirations towards the infinite, this high soaring and deep diving. Both in expression and outlook the new classicism approves the limited, the lucid, the merely small. T. S. Eliot's famous dislike of Milton and of the scale and sumptuosity of the Miltonic style—

* *Speculations.*

53

Wild above rule and art, enormous bliss . . .

can be traced to much the same causes as Hulme's dislike of Romantic 'dampness'. Eliot, who had been much influenced by Hulme and the Imagists—in 1917 he became editor of their periodical *The Egoist*—later made the famous pronouncement that he had become a Royalist in politics, an Anglo-Catholic in religion, and a Classicist in literature. Hulme had connected his anti-romantic theories with such writers as Horace and Pope, of whom he said (in 1913) that 'people nowadays feel a chill when they read them': Eliot located his own classicism in the seventeenth century, and where Hulme had maintained that 'Fancy'—the power of exactly and zestfully describing an object or an experience— was the quality that the new poetry should cultivate, Eliot went on to coin the famous phrase 'unified sensibility' as a criterion for what he held to be best in poetry.

The 'dissociation of sensibility' from which Milton and the Romantics pre-eminently suffered, and from which poetry, in Eliot's view, has never recovered, is brought about by a loss of self-conscious intellectual mastery at every stage of the creative process. So much emerges from Eliot's not very detailed exposition of the phrase. A metaphysical poem may be exceedingly complex; its images, its point of view, its argument, may transform themselves between one sentence and another; but at least the writer is fully in command of the situation. To write such poetry, as Dr Johnson—no friend of the Metaphysicals—remarked, 'it was at least necessary to think'. There is no romantic trance, no surrender to unconscious forces or to impulses only half understood, no surrender of what Valéry called *Moi Clair* to *Moi Trouble*. Eliot, in fact, is employing the term sensibility in the sense of the intelligence, the sensitive faculties, 'the intellect at the tips of the fingers'—not in the sense of the poetic psyche as a whole. Unified sensibility does not mean for Eliot the union of the rational and the irrational faculties in the poetic process. He might say, like Valéry: 'I would rather write something weak, in full consciousness and complete lucidity, than give birth to a masterpiece in a state of trance'. He insists, like Hulme, that any subject is fit for poetry, calling for 'a mechanism of sensibility which can devour any kind of experience', but he never admits or considers the claims of the imagination to possess a unifying power: indeed imagination, with all its romantic associations, is a term of which he is shy. 'Traces of a struggle towards unification of sensibility occur', he concedes, 'in certain passages of Shelley's *Triumph of Life*, and in the second version of Keats's *Hyperion*.' One wonders whether this does not mean simply that both poems were influenced by the style of the *Divine Comedy*, of which Eliot is a great admirer. He passes in silence over the theories of Wordsworth and Shelley, presumably because they had 'revolted against the ratiocinative', and he ignores the efforts of the great Romantics to establish a unity of the imagination and to explore and resolve the mind's qualities. Unified sensibility would appear—significantly, in view of Hulme's pronouncements—to function on an extremely small scale. 'Certain passages . . .' short quotations . . . it is curious to find Eliot accepting without question the normal nineteenth-century Romantic view (of which Poe and Croce are in their different ways exponents) that poetry can be isolated only in short passages, fragments, and single lines.

Whatever Eliot's present views may be, his insistence on unified sensibility should be seen as part of the movement towards classicism which Hulme had begun; and it is difficult not to feel that beside the creative imagination whose enormous, if disorderly, cult in the nineteenth century had produced so much, both Eliot's famous phrase and Hulme's Fancy seem as concepts rather devitalised and prim. In his essay on the Metaphysicals Eliot writes:

> The ordinary man . . . falls in love, or reads Spinoza, and these two experiences have nothing to do with each other, or with the noise of the typewriter or the smell of cooking; in the mind of the poet these experiences are always forming new wholes.

The famous passage is most suggestive, though one may wonder if it goes much beyond Coleridge's remarks on the imagination as reconciling opposite and discordant qualities, but if we turn to Eliot's own poetry, or to the examples of this process that he gives from other modern writers, we find that 'the formation of new wholes' seems to take place in a very mechanical way and according to a formula that might be called more classical or Augustan than Metaphysical.

> *. . . yet there the nightingale*
> *Filled all the desert with inviolable voice*
> *And still she cried, and still the world pursues,*
> *'Jug jug' to dirty ears.*

Extremes—all that the nightingale stands for in poetry and legend, all that dirty ears stand for in life—meet here: sensibility is not so much 'unified' as violently wrenched together. But though the intention may be to absorb and bring into accord the complex notes of modern society, the effect is of a highly deliberate juxtaposition, as deliberate as in, say,

> *And thou, Great Anna, whom three realms obey,*
> *Dost sometimes counsel take, and sometimes tea.*

In Eliot as in Pope the surface play of wit makes a calculated shock upon the reader. There is a resemblance to the Roman-

tic conception of Fancy, the humbler poetic aid whose coun-
ters are fixed associations and responses. As the eighteenth-
century reader became accustomed to the witty mechanism
of contrast—Queen Anne in council and at the tea-table—
and grew to accept it as the normal coinage of poetry, so the
contemporary reader comes to accept the association of
nightingales and dirty ears. Their association even comes to
seem the poetically *conventional* one. Nor is the urbane note
which we should expect from such a convention absent in
Eliot. The poet can first strike an attitude—

> . . . *Scorpion fights against the Sun*
> *Until the Sun and Moon go down*
> *Comets weep and Leonids fly*
> *Hunt the heavens and the plains*
> *Whirled in a vortex that shall bring*
> *The world to that destructive fire*
> *Which burns before the ice-cap reigns.*

—and then disown it as mock-heroic with a shrug, and a
graceful lapse into the colloquial—

> *That was a way of putting it—not very satisfactory:*
> *A periphrastic study in a worn-out poetical fashion.*

The calculated destruction of one mood in the reader in
order, presumably, that he may be able to annex to himself
a wider 'sensibility' seems mechanical and contrived. And
one would rather that poetry were a magical process than
have the magician constantly emerging in his shirt-sleeves
to comment slightingly on the stages of his technique.

It is interesting to find W. B. Yeats emphasising many
years before Eliot coined his phrase that good poetry must
be an expression of the personality as a whole—'blood,
imagination, intellect, running together'. Beside this robust

phrase the neo-classic slogan looks pale: it is as unlikely that
Eliot would employ the word 'blood' in connection with
poetry as that he would employ the term 'imagination'. In
such poems of Eliot's as *Coriolan* and *A Cooking Egg*, disparate fragments, like Spinoza and the smell of cooking,
seem to have been placed side by side to await a process of
fusion which has never occurred. It is illuminating to compare these poems with a section of Yeats's *Vacillation*.

> *My fiftieth year had come and gone,*
> *I sat, a solitary man,*
> *In a crowded London shop,*
> *An open book and an empty cup*
> *On the marble table top.*
> *While on the shop and street I gazed*
> *My body of a sudden blazed;*
> *And twenty minutes more or less*
> *It seemed, so great my happiness,*
> *That I was blessèd and could bless.*

Yeats does not invite us to wonder at the juxtaposition of
tea-shop and mystical experience; he takes it for granted. It
is not for him part of the poem's technical mechanism, its
equipment as a 'new' or 'unified' poem, but simply a feature
of the author's—and therefore of the poem's—total personality.

CHAPTER VI

Organisation or Dispossession?

WE HAVE seen how Hulme divided the requirements of the new classicism into technical reorganisation on the one hand, and a new moral outlook on the other; and how this moral outlook was based on the premises of original sin and the finite nature of man. 'The classical view', he says, 'is absolutely identical with the normal religious attitude . . . part of the fixed nature of man is the belief in the Deity.' And 'it is only by tradition and organisation that anything decent can be got out of man'. With these views Eliot was in complete agreement. In *After Strange Gods* he castigates equally D. H. Lawrence for his worship of sex and darkness, and Thomas Hardy for the 'unwholesome matter' he has to communicate. The new régime, he implies, will require a cleaning up of the romantic heresies, a mopping up of the 'spilt religion' which, said Hulme, romanticism essentially was. By implication, Eliot sees the sources of virtue and the sources of the imagination as lying far apart, for the latter is too closely attached to the irrational powers of the unconscious and the Strange Gods after which society has turned. The imagination has become corrupt: we must rely on the intellect and the 'sensibility'.

This dubiousness about the imagination, the feeling that the hiding-places of man's power were not necessarily allied to virtue, had been felt long before Eliot and Hulme. At an early stage in his thought, Coleridge had rejected the simple eighteenth-century notion that the association of ideas must lead to the realisation of moral truths, and had written that he would try to 'explain the nature of moral evil from the streamy nature of association', when it was passive and uncontrolled. A whole century of romantic abuses is foreshadowed in his words. For Keats, too, the imagination was a neutral spirit, taking as much delight in creating an Iago as an Imogen. But on the whole early Romantic theory assumes the strongest possible connection between the imagination and moral good. Shelley formulated the point most clearly, and it is Shelley who is singled out from among the Romantics for the special disapprobation of Eliot, who regrets that he did not 'live to put his undoubted poetic talent at the service of more acceptable ideas'.

All slogans, explanations, and critical catchphrases by poets and their critics suffer from being almost impossible to relate to the actuality of poetry itself. Thus such terms as 'imagination', 'sensibility', 'poetic truth', etc., can shed very little light on what we get out of poetry or on the reasons why poetry affects us; what they can do is to show us why at certain periods certain poets and their readers thought about poetry as they did. The feeling that poetry should deal with morally acceptable ideas is one that finds expression in many periods of criticism, usually in the argument that intellect and tradition are sounder guides in the making of poetry than are instinct and imagination. The argument may also take the form that poetry has no transmutative power over ideas that are wrong, foolish, or unacceptable to the reader; that what the imagination seizes on as beauty is not necessarily truth. The antithesis thus presents itself between the worth of ideas and the worth of poetry, and it was one that greatly preoccupied the Romantic theorists. Can philosophical truth and poetic truth be made synonymous, or is there an inevitable gap between them? Coleridge thought there was not: and he hoped that Wordsworth's great poem would demonstrate their compatibility, by being the first truly philosophical poem. The reality sadly disappointed him. And with Coleridge's capitulation it became natural for the later Romantics to make the separation between the meaning and ideas in a poem, and the imaginative power with which it makes its impact on the reader. Such a separation would not have seemed possible to Wordsworth, who never conceived his imagination as functioning apart from the full authority of abstract ideas, and who never attempted to liberate his imagination from their service. The great 'visions' of *The Prelude* are always there for a purpose; they are correlated with an abstract argument; and this refusal of Wordsworth to separate vision and idea goes to the fibre of his being and into the very syntax and vocabulary of his poetry. 'Poetry and geometric truth' are for him close allies, and he tells us how in his childhood he was never able to keep the symbols of geometry and algebra apart in his mind from the living spectacle of nature.

For Keats the exact opposite is the case. The division between poetry and philosophy haunted him, and is the theme of most of the critical remarks which he throws off in his letters. 'What the imagination seizes on as beauty must be truth', is his valiant but uneasy sounding attempt to assert a unity between them. In temperament he and Wordsworth are at opposite poles, and where Wordsworth's imagination can hold ideas harmoniously in solution, in Keats's poetry they are apt to be as robust in their abstractness as his images are in their sensuous vividness. The end of the *Ode on a Grecian Urn* is a case in point—

Beauty is truth, truth beauty,—that is all
Ye know on earth, and all ye need to know.

The transition from the world of the poem to the world of intellectual definition is too abrupt, and the reader's consciousness is jolted from one to the other, accepting the poem but hardly able to accept the aphorism without a great deal more clarification of terms, a process in itself absurdly alien to the working of the poetry.

Elsewhere, and much more characteristically, Keats seems to accept poetry as being a purely *natural* activity, like eating or breathing, as opposed to the superior, non-natural field of philosophy or morals. Any 'graceful instinctive attitude' constitutes poetry's material and inspiration, and Keats, using the same significant word, remarks a few sentences earlier in the letter, 'I myself am pursuing the same instinctive course as the veriest human animal you can think of.' He exclaims that 'though a quarrel in the streets is a thing to be hated, the energies displayed in it are fine'—and that these instinctive energies are 'the very thing in which consists poetry; and so it is not so fine a thing as philosophy—for the same reason that an eagle is not so fine a thing as a truth'. 'Not so fine a thing'—though it would be absurd to attach too much critical importance to hasty exclamations in a letter, the underlying attitude of mind—encountered also in the second version of Hyperion—seems to show that Keats accepted the idea of a diminution in the status of poetry, and the fact that it was imprisoned in the domain of the natural. We must remember, too, that though he had most likely not heard them formulated in any philosophic sense, Kantian notions were much in the air at the time through the influence of Coleridge, and Kant had stressed that there is no goodness in Nature as such, that all moral values must be non-natural. But for Keats this 'naturalness' was the very source of vitality—the living creature, whether man or stoat, 'has a purpose and its eyes are bright with it'. And it was the source of all joy and grief as well. His uneasiness about the claims of 'cold philosophy', as he had called it earlier in *Lamia*, and his growing conviction that in that direction lay the important truths and realities, produce crudities and irresolutions which he might have overcome if he had lived: as it is, the gap between poetry and coherent ideas remains—the strength of his poetry is, as Keats puts it, that it was written 'at random—without knowing the bearing of any one assertion or any one opinion'.

Keats's opinions about poetry, easily coarsened and de-sensitised by transmission, had considerable influence in the nineteenth century. Poe's flat pronouncement about the 'de-mands of truth' having nothing to do with poetry is a case in point, while 'the creature has a purpose and its eyes are bright with it' is a remarkably accurate description of the quality that lends its energy and vitality to Browning's verse, the quality of acceptance of human beings for their own sake. It was Keats, perhaps, more than any other of the great Romantics, whose influence tended to dispossess the Roman-tic Imagination, to divorce it from philosophy and ideology, and to confine it to the world of action and sensation. In the nineteenth century the Romantic reaction against tradition and organisation produced the characteristic treatment of emotion and turbulence for its own sake. *Les vrais voyageurs sont ceux-là seuls qui partent pour partir.* To see the results of this process we do not have to go, as Eliot goes, to the Meta-physicals and to Dante: we can see it in two such poets as Spenser and Tennyson—two poets in talent very similar, each with a superb ear and sense of technique, and both, per-haps, somewhat similar in temperament. But if we compare

Spenser's description of the Cave of Despair, in Book I of the *Faerie Queene*, with Tennyson's account of the Lotus Eaters, the difference between the ordered and the dispossessed imagination is extremely clear. Both poets get the utmost out of their material—the poetry of *accidie* could not be better apprehended or more vividly set down—but whereas Spenser knows what he thinks about it, and fits the description into the pattern of traditional ethics to which he adheres, Tennyson merely exploits the imaginative situation as a thing in itself: he is not conditioned to relate his imagination to a settled scheme of thought and belief.

The query now arises—why should he be? Is there any reason why the ordered imagination should be of itself superior to the dispossessed one? Or to put the matter in another way; to be of real importance, must a poet be firmly committed to a view of things which the reader can accept or at least respect? Eliot has said yes, though his affirmation has been tempered by shrewd and sensible qualifications. He concludes that 'I cannot, in practice, wholly separate my poetic appreciation from my personal beliefs'. Much here would depend on how we take the word 'belief', just as—Eliot himself admits—much depends on whether we equate 'believe' with 'fully to understand' in the sense in which we can come to a full understanding of the depth of Shakespeare's *Ripeness is all*, or Dante's *La sua voluntate è nostra pace*. We think of belief as a settled thing, an established groundwork of the mind, whereas romantic poetry deals rather with moods and impulses, with the mind's nomadic and lawless qualities. We do not always feel as Keats or Shelley felt, but at certain times we can enter into their feelings with peculiar intensity: the working of their poetry upon us has not the nature of a calm and sober growth of 'full understanding', but rather of a certain kind of mood or sensation to which the mind at intervals returns, and to which it feels an urge to return. Much here clearly depends on the individual temperament and its bias towards organisation or towards disorder, but in the case of most minds susceptible of poetic experience we may feel that both needs are present; that the settled growth of understanding and respect for what the poet is saying is not in itself more desirable or *better* than a temporary and renewable assent to the mood he induces. To wish that Shelley had 'put his poetry at the service of more acceptable beliefs' is thus to wish that Shelley had been a poet like Dante or Shakespeare: it is critically meaningless because it does not come to grips with the fact of Shelley's poetry at all. Furthermore, however we take the word 'belief' (and Eliot is scrupulous in using it), his conclusion can only cover one sort of poetry—the sort that he might approvingly describe as classical: were we to stretch his conclusion to cover the romantic as well it would have to be: 'we cannot separate our poetic appreciation from our personal beliefs, nor from the moods, prejudices, and emotional requirements that make up the rest of our individuality'.

The possibility of this separation has frequently been asserted, in particular by A. E. Housman in *The Name and Nature of Poetry*. Housman argues that poetry is, as it were, a pure essence, definable only by reference to its physical effects upon the reader, and necessarily mixed up in the language of a poem with such extraneous elements as rational meaning, wit, religion, and so on. For him, the lyrics of Blake and Shakespeare are the purest poetry, because the most 'meaningless'. And so far from desiring poetry to be based on 'acceptable beliefs', he drops a strong hint that he finds a positive antagonism between poetic statement and acceptable belief. The phrase 'Whosoever shall lose his life shall find it' he calls 'the greatest discovery ever made in the moral world', but he emphasises that it is quite outside the sphere of poetry. Compare this attitude with that of T. S. Eliot, for whom *La sua voluntate è nostra pace* is so potent a touchstone because it is not only the finest poetry but is also *literally true* (the italics are his)—and it is one because it is the other.

Eliot and Housman here represent two critical extremes—the former emphasising the position of 'acceptable ideas' in poetry, the latter minimising it. We could, if we liked, regard them as champions of the classic and the romantic point of view. And the dangers inherent in their respective attitudes are easily seen. Housman, whose highest expectation of poetry is that it should be 'ravishing nonsense', would separate the poetic imagination from all dependence on the rest of the intellect: Eliot would emphasise the acceptable at the expense of the imaginative. The *reductio ad absurdum* of Housman's view is Dadaist poetry, while Eliot might in the last resort find himself compelled to place some such unexceptionable sentiment as Pope's

> *We are but parts of one stupendous whole*
> *Whose body Nature is, and God the Soul—*

above Wordsworth's imaginative handling of a similar theme. Criticism like Eliot's may come to connive in a situation where, in Hume's bland phrase, 'the imagination reposes indolently on the idea', and is its obedient servant.

CHAPTER VII

Ghost or Machine?

CRITICAL ATTITUDES towards poetry today have been much influenced by two events: the rediscovery of the Metaphysicals, and the development in the universities of a School of English Literature. There is a connection between the two. As we have seen, Hulme, Pound, and Eliot all emphasised in their various ways what might be called the *scholarship* of poetry. The poet must be precise and he must be learned; 'poetry', says Pound, 'should be as well written as prose', and the implication of the remark (though it turns out to be less arresting than it sounds) is that poetry should be both complex and homely, cerebral, conscientious, and rich in references to a general body of scholarship and idea: that it should, in fact, be possible to get a great deal *out of it*. These requirements were most obviously met by Dryden and the Metaphysical poets, and they are also the kind of qualities which a student of poetry—irrespective of his natural taste and acumen—could most readily perceive, or be induced to perceive. To get a great deal out of a poem is the justification for academic study of it, and an English School tends to set up, in self-defence, professional and mental disciplines which will compare with those required in other subjects. If poetry is to be read as part of an academic course, moreover, the pleasure of reading it becomes altogether too simple a criterion. The analysis and 'evaluation' of poetry must be seen to be an arduous process only to be acquired with practice. A University English tutor has recently announced that our purpose in talking about a poem should be 'not the description of enjoyment but the analysis of meaning'. What disconcerts us here is the implied contrast between the serious business of analysing a poem and the frivolous pleasure of reading it. Such an attitude leaves out of account the function of criticism that most appealed to Dr Johnson. 'It is a good service that one man does another when he tells him his manner of being pleased.'

His manner of being pleased—the contemporary analyst might well retort that this was precisely what the old-time romantic critic would not or could not tell us. Such a critic took refuge, like Lytton Strachey, in a reverential hush— 'these are words not lightly to be mouthed by mortals'—or, like Leslie Stephen, in a deprecatory gesture—'these are mysteries which I shall not here attempt to explain'. When confronted with the actuality of a poem, and how it worked, such critics were indeed inhibited by their sense of its ultimate mystery. They saw it as a ghostly essence, not as a machine which could be taken to pieces, demonstrated, and explained. And for this reason they preferred a mysterious kind of poetry, vague, romantic, suggestive. The analytic critic, on the other hand, prefers poetry with a hard core of reason, with images and metaphors that are exact, and yet carry several shades of meaning that can be paraphrased and reduced by dissection to their smallest constituents.

What effect does the ascendancy of the academic and analytic critic have on modern poetry? One suggestion is that made by Peter Viereck in his epigram *From the Sublime to the Meticulous in Four Stages*.

68

DANTE: We were God's poets.
BURNS: We were the people's poets.
MALLARMÉ: We were poets' poets.
TODAY (*preening himself*): Ah, but *we* are critics' poets.

The sad fact is that it is not difficult to write verse which will stand up to the methods of the analytic critic, which will indeed pass his scrutiny with flying colours. For no matter what qualifications he may make, the analyst involuntarily assumes, in employing his technique, that the poem is a finite, a reducible object; that its component parts can be taken to pieces, shown to be either good or bad, and that a general verdict about the poem can be reached in accordance with these findings. The old-fashioned romantic critic may have been overcome by an excess of respect for the poem's 'ghostliness', but at least this made him aware that, like a human being, it had a life of its own which was ultimately mysterious and irreducible. In a recent number of a critical journal,* a famous phrase of Blake's—*dark Satanic mills*—was subjected to a careful analysis in order to establish its true meaning and to clear up misconceptions arising from careless and subjective readings. (The idea of the one true meaning is a cardinal point of analytic method which has its origin in the academic teaching of poetry: a critical severity is needed to control the vagaries of a vast new potential audience whose reactions, though they usually become docile, are often initially erratic.) The treatment of Blake's phrase gives us a good example of both the good and bad features of close analysis. It revealed three possible lines of interpretation: First, Blake's references to early Druidic ceremonies and myths, for which he often employs the metaphor of mills;

* *Essays in Criticism*, Vol. 2, No. 3.

second, his hatred of industrialism and the tyranny and squalor it had brought; third, his hatred of the established Church—the mills of God. It is not relevant for our enquiry to consider the claims of these interpretations and to agree or disagree with the analyst's verdict—the solution will be found in the journal in question: what concerns us is the attitude to the poetic impact of the phrase which such an analysis suggests. What strikes us, I think, most forcibly is that the analyst is not interested in the quality of Blake's phrase and whether or not it is enjoyable; he exhibits no instinctive knowledge of whether or not the phrase is 'poetic' enough to be worth such attention: the phrase is puzzling enough, that is the criterion. The romantic critic would have tended to take this puzzlement in his stride: his reaction would have been to say 'it's perfect, it's wonderful, and if you can't see that it's no use your reading poetry'. Experience and flair (qualities that analytic critics distrust and, since academic courses are short, cannot afford to dwell upon) would have led him to this conclusion. And there he would let the matter rest. He saw that it was good, whereas the analyst will not admit that it is good until he has seen exactly what is in it, what it may mean, and by the time he has done this the issue has become so fascinating in itself that the quality of the original phrase has become of minor importance.

The danger of analysis, then, is that by ignoring the old conception of *taste*, natural or acquired, it may come more and more to accept what one might call the richly mediocre. Let us imagine a phrase from a modern poem along the lines of Blake's phrase—*those dense ambitious mills*. The taste, flair, or experience of the romantic critic would tell him at once that this was not a good phrase, that it did not work, and he would surely be right. The analyst, on the other hand, would reserve his opinion until he could see what the poet was getting at. He might come to perceive an image, at once visual and intellectual, of complex machinery (dense) and the stupidity of its owners. The regular movements of the machines are cunningly suggested and associated with their owners' blind drive towards success and power. And so on. Already the phrase is becoming poetically respectable by reason of the amount that can be got out of it. The critic's ingenuity is doing duty for the poet's inspiration. But the romantic critic would trust what Owen Barfield, in an extremely illuminating phrase, called 'the felt change of consciousness' that he has when a poem or a phrase of a poem goes home, and which, as I have suggested, is based on his totality of taste and experience. He might speak of it in terms of a mystical apprehension, or a physical *frisson**, or even the effect of a drug, and these metaphors have been assailed by the academic experts as frivolous or inadequate, but the fact remains that the romantic who describes his responses in such terms was less easily taken in than is the contemporary analyst. It is for this reason that we have so much poor contemporary poetry in which the poet, by using his head, has involved and compromised the analyst in a way in which he could not have hoped to take in a romantic critic by using, as it were, a dud drug.

Writing for the critic—the process indicated in Viereck's epigram—thus becomes another feature of contemporary literary self-consciousness. The poetry analyst is in danger of

---

* As Housman did in his famous description of poetic experience in *The Name and Nature of Poetry*. It is worth remembering that Housman in this lecture was consciously challenging the growth of academic criticism. He wrote to his brother afterwards: 'Our doctrinal teachers of youth say it will take twelve years to undo the harm I have done in an hour.' That was twenty-three years ago and, at any rate in the universities, the harm seems by now to have been undone pretty effectively!

performing the same disservice for modern verse as the psychoanalyst has for the modern novel. If symbolism is, as C. S. Lewis has put it, 'a mode of thought', whose relevance and power have their sources in the unconscious, it follows that author and reader cannot without loss of power parallel this obscure thought process on the level of hypostasis and reason. But once author and reader have been made conscious of how these processes are presumed to work, it is difficult for them to do anything else. The novelist's original language of myth and symbol is thus being continually glossed, or dubbed—while it is actually in the process of creation by the writer or of appreciation by the reader— into the more commonplace language of the interpretative consciousness. It is unlikely that Herman Melville would have conceived of Moby Dick if he had been familiar with Freud, or that Hardy could have written the great scene in *Far from the Madding Crowd* in which Sergeant Troy shows Bathsheba the sword exercise, if he had thought of it as a piece of sexual symbolism.

Similarly, as cerebration and analysis invade modern poetry, the ghost, the unexplained vitality which makes the poem a living thing, and which the poet himself cannot account for or justify, gives way to a careful fitting and testing of all parts of the machine in order that it may pass the critic's scrutiny. Where both poem and novel are concerned, the creator tends to become the prey of his own and his critic's intelligence. And for poetry the solution must lie in a partial return to the critical premises of romanticism, in the whole-hearted submission to a poetic experience before we begin to analyse it. Certainly we should not undervalue the advantages to be gained from the close and careful reading of a poem, and from the examination of its difficulties and its component effects. But such a reading should be a sec-

ondary process and should modify our more instinctive reaction to the life of the poem, not determine it. A poem is
both ghost and machine, and though a machine can be dis-
mantled and demonstrated without reverence, a ghost is still
entitled to be treated with something of the old romantic
awe.

PART TWO

THE
ROMANTIC
SURVIVAL

CHAPTER VIII

W. B. Yeats

IN THE previous pages I have tried to show how romantic ideas, developing and proliferating over the course of more than a century, affected the writing and the reading of imaginative literature. We have seen how the novel was transformed, becoming the dominant creative form under the impulse of romantic egotism and individualism, and showing the all-important and all-interesting 'I' creating his environment or at odds with it; how 'counter-reformations' like that of Hulme and Eliot sought to discredit romanticism and reverse its tendencies; and, most important of all, how the universe of romantic poetry began to shrink, diminishing into the mental world of the symbolists, or into a catalogue of stock romantic properties.

I shall now take three poets—Yeats, Auden, and Dylan Thomas—in whose work can be seen many of the aspects of romanticism which have been discussed and who constitute the greatest and most interesting exponents of a new sort of romantic revival. In their poetry the romantic horizons have expanded again, the original vitality and breadth of the movement have been restored. As we examine the ways in which this has been brought about, we shall see that only in the context of romantic thought and theory, both its strength and its weakness, can the size of their poetry be properly appreciated and its positive qualities understood. All are poets who found romanticism at a low ebb, and its legacy rather a liability than an asset, but who were able to rediscover its original scope and richness.

How great their achievement is can be seen more clearly if we consider for a moment two poets, not less talented than they, who also came to their powers at the time of greatest romantic meagreness and devitalisation—A. E. Housman and Walter de la Mare. At first sight no two poets could appear more different. Housman the classical scholar, whose taut, neat verses with their stoical and Horatian overtones challenge, as H. W. Garrod has remarked, the romanticism of his critical utterances; and Walter de la Mare, whose poems, although singularly varied in their moods of joy and disquiet, have always the same longing behind them for

> *A beauty beyond earth's content,*
> *A hope—half memory. . . .*

But both, with their extreme narrowness of range, seem engaged in keeping alive the last flicker of the ideal flame; neither can accept what they see in the world, with its horrifying abundance and complexity. Feeling only

> *Deadly disquiet*
> *Of this homeless place*

they look for innocence and perfection in dream and in childhood—

> *The happy highways where I went*
> *And cannot come again.*

Their inspiration has the same source although they differ in their response to its appeal. 'The sweet cheat gone', de la Mare turns to what is left with a patient, haunted acceptance. His hope is in an ideal Platonic universe,

And all I love
In beauty cries to me,
'We but vain shadows
And reflections be' . . .

Life offers most at its edges—'the actual realest on the verge of sleep'. Even the Iago whom the poet imagines shares his preoccupation and longs for

One fragile hour of heedless innocence
And then, Farewell, and the incessant grave.

By contrast Housman's tone is one of wry, neat mockery at himself for cherishing romantic yearnings and illusions but also at the reader for taking pleasure in this kind of thing. He makes a distinction between a licensed nostalgia in poetry and the need for keeping a stiff upper lip in the actual business of living; and the irony of this contrast is paralleled by the contrast between the romantic content of his poems and the military precision of their form. One suspects that his critical emphasis on poetry as 'ravishing nonsense' arises from his disbelief in the substantiality of what he writes about: romantic feelings become equated with nonsense and unreality, and yet such unreality is all that poetry has to work on. In Housman the romantic and the Stoic ideals have come incongruously together and agreed to part human experience rigorously between them, and the partnership, incongruous as if Wordsworth had elected to spend half the year among the mountains of the lake district and half in the polite society of a London salon, reveals how fundamental Housman's irony is and how shrivelling in its effect on the dimension of poetry.

In spite of the differences between them, therefore, both poets show how narrow the romantic field has become.

Even innocence, the positive quality which de la Mare touches on so continually and delicately, can only be evoked in the frailest and most oblique of images—'the secret of the child, the bird, the night'. The human nature of 'God's spy', who has apprehensions of innocence and can catch something of the mystery of things, is never indicated, indeed cannot be, for to anchor him firmly to the everyday earth as Kierkegaard anchored his 'Knight of the Faith', who looked like a tax collector and enjoyed his dinner of sheep's head, would be to destroy what had come to seem romanticism's last stronghold in the aloof and disembodied and forlorn.

It is interesting to compare this perception of innocence and the treatment of it with Auden's. In senses which we shall presently discuss, Auden's poetry is no less under the romantic influence than is de la Mare's, but between the two poets romanticism has anchored itself to the earth once more. Whatever we may think of Auden's idea of innocence—and it may seem a suspiciously stylised one—it touches actuality at all points, not only 'at the edges'. 'God's spy', the man who knows, is an enigmatic figure, but his untouched, unsoiled nature—which the older poet conveyed in terms of mystery and intangibility—is here held down firmly to the everyday and the commonplace,

> *The only difference that could be seen*
> *From those who'd never risked their lives at all*
> *Was his delight in details and routine:*
>
> *For he was always glad to mow the grass,*
> *Pour liquids from large bottles into small,*
> *Or look at clouds through bits of coloured glass.*

The great man about whom 'A shilling life will give you all

the facts' has a vision of the same sort of innocence, and 'sighed for one',

> *Who, say astonished critics, lived at home;*
> *Did little jobs about the house with skill*
> *And nothing else; could whistle; would sit still*
> *Or potter round the garden; answered some*
> *Of his long marvellous letters but kept none.*

Those details, 'potter', 'little jobs', 'mowing the grass', etc., do their best to convey an impression of the absolutely humdrum that is none the less in some way illuminated and mysterious.

Although in Auden's poetry, then, there is the same nostalgia for the innocent, the remote, and the mysterious, these romantic qualities are differently located and are written about in a totally different spirit. In asking ourselves how this change occurred the first name we think of is that of Yeats. Yeats, like de la Mare, inherited a romantic sensibility that had become exiguous and reverential, and was only a little expanded by his treatment of Irish legend and folklore. He decided to change his style and outlook, and this decision —and his ability to carry it through—mark both the abandonment of the old romantic properties and their successful extension and resettlement.

So much detailed and authoritative criticism of Yeats's poetry has recently appeared that a further contribution might well appear unnecessary. We have had studies of his personality, his symbolic system, his mysticism, and his changes of style. Many of his poems have been carefully analysed, and their obscurities explained by reference to his multifarious interest in legend and magic, the Irish scene, painting, historical ideology. The influence of the French Symbolists, and of Swinburne and the poets of the *fin-de-siècle*, has been duly noted. But all this criticism, emphasising as it does one or other of the aspects of Yeats's work, has an oddly fragmented quality. Disclaimers are frequent: critics who interpret his magic system are careful to insist that the excellence of his poetry is in no way dependent on it, and those who have commented on the peculiarity of his ideas, or analysed the progression of his thought, usually conclude that his greatness in some way lies outside them.

By implication, therefore, Yeats's achievement remains parcelled out under such heads as his style, his metrical and colloquial energy, and the aesthetic splendour of his great symbols such as Byzantium and the Tower. His vision as a whole, his world as a whole, is not taken seriously and not allowed as the real measure of his greatness. The unspoken critical verdict is that in Yeats's case the whole is not greater than the sum of its parts—that it is in fact a good deal smaller. And this is ironic, because Yeats was more consciously preoccupied than other romantic writers by the desire for a poetic vision that should be total, all-inclusive, while remaining outside any official system, religious or ideological —ways to live and think by which Yeats might dally with and draw upon, but which he always ended by insisting, 'are not my ways'. This refusal to commit himself is characteristic of an attitude which sought on the one hand to escape from the unworldly mind regions of the Symbolists, and on the other, not to become 'public' in the opprobrious sense of accepting the values and beliefs of the age and making poetry out of them. Yeats, like Wordsworth, determined to be a traveller whose tale was only of himself, but how was that self to be kept interesting, to be kept both apart from life and engaged in it? That, for Yeats, was the romantic poet's dilemma, and his whole development can best be seen as a series of brilliant and self-conscious expedients for solving it. The purpose and the will behind these expedients give a coherence and a vision to all the poetry, once we have understood them.

Crudely speaking, the criterion of romantic success is to imagine a world different from anyone else's. This may be done self-consciously, by a perpetual, strong-willed juggling with abstracts and events, as in the case of Yeats; or instinctively, by the natural cast of mind and imagination, as in the case of Walter de la Mare or—to take a very different example—Dylan Thomas. But all romantics are Robinson Crusoes, alone on a wide wide sea, and driven by 'le coeur Robinson' to produce their own version of reality. In his youthful experiences Wordsworth had perceived 'modes of being' which before him had hardly been conceived of as possessing independent significance and value, but he came eventually to accept and to live by beliefs of a much more conventional kind. The separation foreshadowed between the poetic apprehension and a process of coming to terms with life was one that haunted Yeats. And, paradoxically, he sees the way out in terms of becoming a complex personality instead of a simple one; if the self cannot always retain one poetry-giving vision before it, it must become many different selves. It must cultivate disciplines, attitudes, forms and models that it would not take to naturally, *personae* uncongenial to it—and all must be co-ordinated and carried through by the force of the poet's will. He blames Wordsworth for his singleness, remarking: 'if we cannot imagine ourselves as different from what we are, we cannot impose a discipline upon ourselves.' If his *raison d'être*, to create his own individual vision, is to endure, the romantic poet must submit to artificial disciplines and exercises which will enable him to 'embòdy reality' in his verse even if he does not perceive it in the world or by believing in any religion or ideology. 'For'—as Yeats puts it—

> *though heart might find relief*
> *Did I become a Christian man and choose for my belief*
> *What seems most welcome in the tomb—play a predestined part—*
> (Vacillation)

such a capitulation would be the end of him as a poet. Not that he cannot develop systems and ideologies of his own— Yeats spawned them like a salmon—but he must be at every moment prepared to abandon them or turn them inside out, and continue in a state of 'fruitful uncertainty'.

Keats's phrase is illuminating. For there is a sense, and a rather absurd sense to those to whom the attempt seems misguided, in which Yeats seems to be trying to achieve negative capability by numbers, to become 'a Proteus of the fire and flood' by means of a kind of athletic technique. If we think artificiality on this scale insuperably distasteful, we cannot be in complete sympathy with Yeats's outlook. But if we understand its origins and the premises on which it rests, there is no reason why we should find it more distasteful than—say—the attempts of Spenser, Sidney and their contemporaries to create artificially a new English poetry. Full appreciation of Yeats is hampered by preconceptions about the nature of poetry which are, ironically enough, based on the very romantic ideals with which he is so fundamentally in sympathy. We expect a great romantic poet to exhibit an inclusive and individual vision; but we also expect this to be in some way 'natural', to have developed spontaneously in the context of his creative power, and to emerge like the leaves on the tree. His *poetry*, we think, may be artificial, for poetry is after all a formal art, but his *vision* must be spontaneous. But Yeats will not admit this. His vision and his poetry are equally artificial, equally the product of theory and the will, or, as he would have said, equally the product of 'blood, imagination, intellect, running together'. In his desire for the romantic wholeness of vision and poetic personality Yeats is prepared to throw over the whole romantic conception of the ideal, and the spontaneous overflow.

It follows from his idea of the inflexible wholeness of artificiality that there must be nothing *outside* poetry which either causes it to flow or prevents it. Abstract thought is dangerous, he sees; he deplores his tendency to think in theories and abstractions, and he is humble when the young James Joyce accuses him of generalising, and of talking more like a man of letters than a poet. What is to be done? He cannot submit to abstraction, but he will not banish it either, for that would rob poetry of its inclusiveness. He must artificialise it, then: he must marry the abstract attitude with the rhythmical one, so that it becomes 'an *effect* of verse [italics mine], spoken by a man almost rhythm-drunk, to give the apex of long-mounting thought'. Youth and its fervours, the golden age of romantic inspiration, is to be particularly distrusted. He has seen too many of

> *The best-endowed, the elect,*
> *All by their youth undone,*
> *All, all, by that inhuman*
> *Bitter glory wrecked.*
>
> *But I have straightened out* (he goes on)
> *Ruin, wreck, and wrack;*
> *I toiled long years and at length*
> *Came to so deep a thought*
> *I can summon back*
> *All their wholesome strength.*

85

We do not hear what the 'great thought' was, and we do not want to. The poem is not about it, but—as so often with Yeats's poems—about his feelings on his art and what has gone into it, about his art itself. The best artificial subject is the artistic process, and how this process works upon—

> *Poet's imaginings*
> *And memories of love,*
> *Memories of the words of women.*
> *All those things whereof*
> *Man makes a superhuman*
> *Mirror-resembling dream.*

> (*The Tower*)

'A superhuman mirror-resembling dream'—the phrase goes a long way towards summing up what Yeats thought that poetry should be. And poetry should never be produced, Yeats feels, by some external emotion which remains more powerful than the poetry itself. War and the emotions it aroused, since these could not be artificialised and remained outside the poet's grasp, were unsuitable. They could never be fully comprehended in the 'blood, imagination and intellect'. We may be distressed by his attitude to Wilfred Owen's poetry, which he calls 'all blood, dirt, and sucked sugar-stick', but we have to admit that according to his own philosophy Yeats could not have accepted Owen. 'The poetry is in the pity'—Owen's poignantly accurate description of how his verse was written would have made no sense to Yeats. How could poetry reside in some large general emotion outside the author's scope and control? How could the poetry be anywhere outside the poet? It is an inflexible application of the romantic egotism that the

poet's universe must be purely his own. War must be a
factor in the poet's consciousness, not a public emotion. Both
the justice and the injustice of Yeats's claim can be seen if we
compare a verse of his with what are perhaps the finest lines
Owen wrote. The subject is a dead soldier.

> *Whether his deeper sleep lie shaded by the shaking*
> *Of great wings, and the thoughts that hung the stars,*
> *High-pillowed on calm pillows of God's making*
> *Above these clouds, these rains, these sleets of lead,*
> *And these winds' scimitars;*
> *—Or whether yet his thin and sodden head*
> *Confuses more and more with the low mould,*
> *His hair being one with the grey grass*
> *And finished fields of autumns that are old. . . .*
> *Who knows? Who hopes? Who troubles? Let it pass.*
> *He sleeps. He sleeps less tremulous, less cold,*
> *Than we who must awake, and waking, say Alas!*
>
> *(Asleep)*

The sentiment of pity here is so deep that it does appear to
leave the poetry behind, to submerge the critical faculty, and
to blind the reader to the inferior, Flecker-like image of 'the
thoughts that hung the stars' and to the precise and almost
Shakespearean strangeness of *Confuses*, and *finished fields*.
There is something 'extra-poetic' in the very implausibility
of the picture suggested by the literary flavour of the images
in the first part, while those of the second come from the
heart of an experience. And the poem seems to transcend
both the good and the bad in it. The poet's indifference to
the great question asked depends upon his being too deeply
involved, not in the poetry, but in the situation which has
produced the poetry. It is not an indifference, as Yeats's

would be, contrived of set purpose in the interests of the poem. We might put beside Owen a stanza from Yeats's poem *Nineteen Hundred and Nineteen*.

> *Now days are dragon-ridden, the nightmare*
> *Rides upon sleep: a drunken soldiery*
> *Can leave the mother, murdered at her door,*
> *To crawl in her own blood, and go scot-free;*
> *The night can sweat with terror as before*
> *We pieced our thoughts into philosophy,*
> *And planned to bring the world under a rule,*
> *Who are but weasels fighting in a hole.*

At first sight there seems to be, if not pity, at least a straight-forward, 'non-poetic' indignation in these lines. But as we complete our reading, we see that Yeats has subdued the image of the murdered mother in the interests of his own vision of the times, which is at once more withdrawn, more comprehensive, and more personal. The very word *crawl*, joining up with the image in the last line, suggests some meaningless turbulence of animal suffering (comparable to the images of such suffering in *King Lear* to which we are introduced by Lear's desire 'to crawl unburdened towards death'). This is contrasted with the rule of art and thought. Their coincidence in the poet's mind, his ability to move from one to the other with comprehension but without emotion or regret, makes the vision peculiarly *his*: past order and present anarchy both seem, for the moment, to exist solely in order that Yeats may perceive how to fasten on to the contrast and make poetry out of it.

The determination to be himself lies at the back of Yeats's famous rejection of his early manner and of the conventional handling of Irish Mythology. This kind of poetry is not his real self but only 'a coat'—

> *Covered with embroideries*
> *Out of old mythologies*
> *From heel to throat;*
> *But the fools caught it,*
> *Wore it in the world's eyes*
> *As though they'd wrought it.*
> *Song, let them take it,*
> *For there's more enterprise*
> *In walking naked.*

The lines have often been quoted to illustrate his change of style, but it is more important that they show his determination not to draw any longer upon what had become a common stock of romantic material. His vision must be his own; 'Walking naked' was being Yeats, and this ability to disown old selves in his search for new techniques of becoming a completely individual poetic self distinguishes him from the other poets of the period even before his work had begun to show its immense superiority over theirs. How completely he identified himself with his poetry is seen in the verse he wrote after receiving criticisms of the changes he had made in his early work.

> *They that hold that I do wrong*
> *Whenever I remake a song*
> *Should recollect what is at stake:*
> *It is myself that I remake.*

'How can we know the dancer from the dance?' he ends the poem *Among School-Children,* and the image of the dancer, so rapt among the many figures she makes that she seems a part of them, is one of his formal symbols. This fanatical identification goes far to explain how Yeats could continue to develop as he did, continuing to mirror every fresh experience, physical and mental, that age brought him. His inconsistency is a natural consequence of this development. High passion and humorous earthy lust, bravado and pathos, public indignation and private self-mockery—all are compatible in the creating mind that will not commit itself to anything but the poetry it can make of them.

The comparison with Wilfred Owen has shown the limitations of the process: poetry is life and life is poetry, and the very completeness of the circle makes a kind of closed and insulated aesthetic. Although there is nothing left out—indeed because there is nothing left out—existence outside the circle seems for Yeats irrelevant, meaningless, unimportant. There are no mysteries, no profundities outside, which—as Owen obscurely felt about pity—poetry can touch but not transmute; nothing which poetry must seek to become a part of, rather than to absorb into itself. The doctrines of Symbolism, that logical ending to romantic 'otherness', had had a deep influence upon Yeats. Mallarmé had said: *Tout au monde existe pour aboutir à un livre.* But for Mallarmé the world was the mind, the ultimate romantic region in which poetry had its genesis and being. Yeats's self-appointed task was to bring this Symbolist absolutism back to the world of action and event, to make the outer world its province. But the same uncompromising theory, the world for art's sake, underlies its purpose. 'Words alone are certain good', he echoes Mallarmé in one of his earliest poems, and the same principle dominated him to the end. The influence of Symbolism was strengthened by that of Pater and the English aesthetes, and Yeats was the one disciple who was both serious and successful enough to give meaning to the famous passage about 'burning always with a hard gem-like flame':

in the context of his mature manner the phrase acquires point. Of his association with Arthur Symons, Yeats records that 'we always discussed life at its most intense moment'. Matthew Arnold had called religion 'morality touched by emotion': the goal of aesthetic behaviour was short and intense periods of emotion untouched by morality.

Compared with this conception of the artist, the influence of the actual theory of the Symbol on Yeats's work is comparatively unimportant. It exercises nothing like such a strong effect on the nature of the poetry as does the aesthetic background of late Romanticism. Yeats, as we have said, brings Romanticism back to earth, but he pays the price of making himself and his poetry the measure of all things. So, it may be argued, do all romantic poets, but never before with Yeats's self-conscious deliberation. Towards other poets and their experiences he maintained a careful policy of exclusion or non-comprehension. 'It may be a way', he would reiterate, 'but it is not my way'. The paradox of his later years is that though he followed keenly the course of politics and literary fashion, and read Spengler, Jung, Russell, and other thinkers, he remained an isolated figure, whose vision, though it drew on these materials, remained too completely his own to seem anything but outlandish, reactionary, and uncongenial to the younger writers. 'Like Balzac', he wrote in a letter, 'I know no one who shares the premises from which I work'. T. S. Eliot, reviewing *The Cutting of an Agate* in *The Athenaeum*, adopts a tone of extreme disapproval, and speaks of Yeats's vision as 'egotistic and crude'. Eliot, we remember, was already seeking to commit himself to values which could not be subdued into the aesthetic vision of the individual. W. H. Auden, writing in *The Kenyon Review*, remarked that Yeats's rhythm and the conversational power of his poetry had had tremendous influence, but his vision, none. While agreeing with Auden's tribute to the influence of Yeats's style, we may wonder whether the latter's view of what the poet should be has really had so little effect. Auden himself goes on to say that Yeats turned the occasional poem into a *genre* of real importance: and he implies that this was done by Yeats's ability to endow his friends, his family and house and daily life with such an urgent and sumptuous poetic existence. The small doings of his friends—Mrs French and her butler, Henry Middleton and his quiet house in a Sligo suburb—become as incalculably significant as the deeds of epic heroes. 'All the Olympians, a thing never known again.' Simply by virtue of the relationship, Yeats's grandfather joins the 'half legendary men', the company of Pearse and Cuchulain, Parnell and Casement. Nor is there anything laughable in this association: Yeats's total absence of self-consciousness, the grandeur of his insulation, if one may so call it, makes his valuation of these personalities and happenings completely convincing. Now Auden's own poetic vision, where it is most effective and compelling, seems to owe much to Yeats's example in this respect. As we shall see, Auden succeeds just as effectively as Yeats in endowing the apparent trivialities of life with a mysterious significance, a kind of esoteric harmony, and this vision is just as uncommitted to an allegiance *outside its own existence as poetry* as is Yeats's own. This particular romantic survival, in fact, depends on the poet's success in creating a world constructed of simple recognisable materials —friends, houses, careers, cars, gasometers, the Communist Party—but transformed by a fine conspiracy of style and manner into something *eo ipso*, an aesthetic world in which, as Auden puts it, 'what delights us is just that it neither is nor could possibly become one in which we could breathe or behave'. Auden, like Yeats, has read all the latest theories, and is able to absorb a great deal more contemporary detail into his private magical universe. But it is a universe of essentially the same kind, insulated, unique, and founded on the same original rejection by the Symbolists of the nineteenth-century material world in favour of a mind-created structure.

Whereas Yeats identifies himself and his poetry completely with one another, Auden sets up—most illuminatingly—a barrier between the man who is subject to the laws and limitations of being in the world, and the poet who is not. As poet, 'playing God with words', he is free; as a human being he must live with and for other human beings: and he must never confuse his two rôles. We *may* write poetry, but we *must* live; and Auden has said that the poet's prayer should be: 'Let me write so well that I shall no longer want to.' This would have seemed great nonsense to Yeats, for whom the life of the poet, and his poetry, were one and the same. But we can see how the progression has logically occurred. From the Symbolist's rejection of the external world we move to Yeats's acceptance of it—provided that it can be absorbed wholly by the poet's egocentricity—and thence to Auden's division of the egocentric poet from the man who must commit himself, though not his poetry, to theories and beliefs about the real world.

In the next chapter we shall see how this affects Auden's poetry. He is deeper in Yeats's debt than he is aware, and the debt is of a peculiarly valuable kind: indeed both poets owe their success very largely to what they have been able to make on the basis of the old Symbolist position. But Auden dislikes and distrusts Yeats's deliberate grooming of the poetic personality until it is trained to assume any kind of mask or attitude. And he dislikes the magic. 'A. E. Housman's pessimistic stoicism seems to me to be nonsense too'—

he remarks of it—'but at least it is the kind of nonsense that can be believed in by a gentleman.' Overt association with magic is ungentlemanly, but, as we shall see, in Auden himself magic is confessedly only just beneath the surface.

We might classify the technique whereby Yeats seeks to attain a wide and intense poetic vision under three heads— the Mask, the Conversation, and the Symbol. Of these the first is the most continuously important. Yeats began to develop his theory of it about four years before *Responsibilities*, appearing in 1914, introduced the new style. In his diary in 1910, he calls the Mask idea 'an imaginative Saturnalia that one may forget reality'. The connection with Romantic escape and *Poésie des Départs* is clear: but, as Yeats implies later in his diary, one can best free oneself from a humdrum connivance in materialistic society, not by escaping from it, but by adopting one after another some of its more graphic and energetic appearances. 'I think all happiness in life depends on having the energy to assume the mask of some other self, that all joyous and contented life is a rebirth as something not oneself, something created in a moment and perpetually renewed: in playing a game like that of a child where one loses the infinite pain of self-realisation.' The energy and purpose of the adult, the unreflecting passion of a child—can they be made compatible? To make them so will be one of the functions of the mask. But in phrases like 'forget reality' and 'the pain of self-realisation' we see how the mask idea, at least in its early stages, is a method for getting away from something, getting away from *being* into a world of acting and poetry. Yeats puts the theory into practice in his cycle of poems called

Upon a Dying Lady. The lady was Mabel Beardsley, Aubrey Beardsley's sister, who was dying of cancer.

> *She is playing like a child*
> *And penance is the play,*
> *Fantastical and wild*
> *Because the end of day*
> *Shows her that someone soon*
> *Will come from the house and say—*
> *Though play is but half done—*
> *'Come in and leave the play'.*

Yeats puts himself into the position of the dying lady, and decides that 'play' is the appropriate Mask to confront death. 'We have naught for death but toys.' And we see at once how entirely he has usurped the position of Mabel Beardsley. Actual person as she is, and painfully actual as is her fate, she is for Yeats the occasion to try out a mask which will enable him to absorb her fate, as it were, and remove it from any reality outside that of his poetic vision. 'Penance is the play' —Yeats neither shows nor wishes to show any comprehension of what the act of penance might mean to a Roman Catholic who believed in the Church. But this is not an adverse criticism. Mabel Beardsley is for Yeats what Edward King was for Milton when he wrote *Lycidas*—an occasion for a poem about the author and his views: the doctrine of the mask has brought this kind of romanticism back to an almost seventeenth-century position of rhetorical detachment.

The 'forgetting of reality' has dubious overtones when it is stated as a theory, and we cannot help remembering them when, at the end of his poetic career, Yeats is still speaking through the same Mask of play before death, though now his pronouncement no longer requires an actor but has taken a more generalised and authoritative form.

> All perform their tragic play,
> There struts Hamlet, there is Lear,
> That's Ophelia, that Cordelia;
> Yet they, should the last scene be there,
> The great stage curtain about to drop,
> If worthy their prominent part in the play,
> Do not break up their lines to weep.
> They know that Hamlet and Lear are gay;
> Gaiety transfiguring all that dread.

The tone of *Lapis Lazuli* introduces us to another important Mask—the Mask of violence. Again, its purpose may be the 'forgetting of reality'—in this case the tameness of modern times. 'Some years ago', he writes in *Per Amica Silentia Lunae*, 'I began to believe that our culture, with its doctrine of sincerity and self-realisation, made us gentle and passive, and that the Middle Ages and the Renaissance were right to found theirs upon the imitation of Christ, or of some classic hero. St Francis and Cesare Borgia made themselves over-mastering creative persons by turning from the mirror to meditation upon a mask.' Insincerity, Yeats implies, is a necessary condition of this enlargement of the personality: the word would carry no pejorative overtone for him, but would be used in a neutral and technical way, as if it were a term like 'alliteration' or 'baroque'. Insincerity would thus be the skill involved in expressing oneself like St Francis in one poem or part of a poem, and like Cesare Borgia in another. Again we note with what superb self-consciousness Yeats has called in a seventeenth-century concept—the sub-ordination of the author to the poem's immediate forensic purpose—to redress the balance of the Symbolist position.

Yeats was a diffident and timid young man, and his decision to alter his personality in the direction of greater toughness and arrogance was strengthened by the controversies
that marked his increasing involvement in public life. It was
Cesare Borgia rather than St Francis who was useful to him
here. In 1910 he had a complicated quarrel with Edmund
Gosse, and in *Responsibilities* he makes use of the uproar
about *The Playboy of the Western World*. Synge was a close
friend, and Synge had said that before poetry could become
human again it must become brutal: his own ballads were
written to demonstrate the point. 'I have always held that a
model is necessary to style', wrote Yeats towards the end of
his life, and Synge seems to have provided at this stage a
model for the Mask of violence. With his remarkable gift
for discerning a possible self in his conception of a friend,
Yeats saw in Synge a hypothetically Yeatsian intensity. Like
Mabel Beardsley, Synge becomes an aspect of Yeats—

A portion of my mind and life, as it were,

as Yeats was to write later about his friends. He speaks of
Synge 'accepting death and dismissing life' in *Deirdre*, 'with
a gracious gesture', and the comment seems appropriate only
to Yeats: about Synge it is not very illuminating.

Not that the Mask technique grew entirely out of a process of modelling on other personalities. Ezra Pound appears
to have been for Yeats, as he was for many others, a technical rather than a personal influence, and from 1914 on-
wards Yeats learnt much from Pound's theories of historical
expression, just as on the dramatic side he learnt much from
Pound's interest in the Japanese *Noh* plays. Reviewing
Pound's *Propertius*, T. S. Eliot remarked on 'the peculiarity
of expressing oneself through historical masks', and on the
necessity the modern poet found 'to collate his disguises'. To

collate his disguises—the phrase sums up with considerable accuracy Yeats's own aims at this time. He had no concern with verbal consistency in matters of critical definition, but he observes the greatest consistency in the handling of his chosen technique. He might have said with Valéry, *se connaître n'est que se prévoir, et se prévoir aboutit à jouer un rôle,* but whereas Valéry (whom Yeats found unsympathetic) affected a position of philosophical lucidity in his search for himself, Yeats saw the process as something shifting and changing, something in which the formal hypostasis of definition should never be the goal. He meditated his future selves as a novelist meditates his characters: his great admiration for Balzac indicates how sympathetic he found the novelist's task of creating widely different people from his own intuition and experience. In response to his father's demand for a tale 'about real people', he wrote the early novel *John Sherman*, in which the dreamy and ineffective Sherman is contrasted with the efficient High Church curate, Howard. The two sides of the poet, or rather two possibilities for him, are imagined in action in much the same way as Goncharov imagined two conflicting types in his novel *Oblomov*. In the making of his artificial world Yeats drew—as much as on any source—on the nineteenth-century fictional tradition which had risen out of the Romantic movement. He admired the detachment with which the romantic novelist could create characters who externalised the conflicting energies and desires inside himself. 'If Balzac had written with a very personal, very highly-coloured style, he would have always drowned his inventions with himself.' Yeats had not the novelist's peculiar power of creation, but he could make use of the novelist's creative technique. Sherman and Howard are followed by the tough, violent Robartes— 'more of a mask than face: debauchee, saint and peasant', as

Yeats describes him—and the contemplative Aherne, a Catholic on the verge of being a Dominican. Cuchulain and Conchobar are a similar kind of self and anti-self, or mask and anti-mask, both ideals of activity, but the former a stylish, disengaged hero, and the latter a responsible and sober king who wants, like Tennyson's King Arthur, 'to leave a strong and settled country to my children', while Cuchulain goes out magnificently to fight the waves.

So Yeats resolved 'the antinomies', as he liked—borrowing a phrase of Blake's—to call these extremes of possibility. Sometimes he sees himself as wearing the Mask of calm and quiet, and Maud Gonne that of turbulence and splendour.

> *Have I not seen the loveliest woman born*
> *Out of the mouth of plenty's horn,*
> *Because of her opinionated mind*
> *Barter that horn and every good*
> *By quiet natures understood*
> *For an old bellows full of angry wind.*
> > (*Prayer for my Daughter.*)

Like Conchobar, Yeats the family man desired for his children all the order and peace of civilisation, for

> *How but in custom and in ceremony*
> *Are innocence and beauty born?*

but as a poet he could not commit himself to these values. He must be Cuchulain as well. And since the possibility of heroic action is not for him, a heroism of style must take its place, a convention of violence which can penetrate at will into the most apparently pacific things. The face of nature herself becomes charged with this violence of epithet. Yeats writes of 'the 'outrageous stars', 'the bursting dawn', 'the headlong light', 'raving autumn', 'the murderous innocence

of the sea'. It is as if even the simplest things had their Mask
and Anti-Mask, and could be seen in either role. The first
line of the poem *On those who hated the Playboy of the
Western World,*

> *Once when midnight smote the air,*

sets the tone of the poem with the conscious vigour of its
verb. Yeats would have delighted in the famous metaphor
from *The Ancient Mariner,*

> *The sun's rim dips, the stars rush out,*
> *At one stride comes the dark,*

and would have appreciated how the dynamic function of
Nature in Coleridge's poem, both breaking and making the
human actors, was mirrored in the words. Yeats does not
always employ violence so functionally—'outrageous stars'
is a decorative and mechanical use of the strong word—but
in the opening poem of *The Winding Stair* the violence is
employed with an extraordinary subtlety.

> *The light of evening, Lissadell,*
> *Great windows open to the south,*
> *Two girls in silk kimonos, both*
> *Beautiful, one a gazelle.*
> *But a raving autumn shears*
> *Blossom from the summer's wreath. . .*

The effect of the word *raving* here depends upon its detached
prolepsis. All the other words—*light, silk, Lissadell*—suggest
tranquillity and calm: and the girls in this serene setting are
treated with an elaborate courtesy and forbearance—*raving*
is not applied to them.

> *Dear shadows, now you know it all,*
> *All the folly of a fight*
> *With a common wrong or right.*

But in spite of this politeness and beauty, the strong, almost coarse, censure implied by the early adjective (in one of his last poems Yeats writes of *that raving slut*) still prevails, and emphasises the virulence of the emotions that are now at rest.

Some of the most effective employments of the Mask are when Yeats hesitates, or affects to hesitate, between two of them,

> *The intellect of man is forced to choose*
> *Perfection of the life, or of the work,*

—as he states it theoretically. In the *Meditations in Time of Civil War* the contrast has a particular urgency.

> *A brown Lieutenant and his men*
> *Half-dressed in national uniform*
> *Stand at my door, and I complain*
> *Of the foul weather, hail and rain,*
> *A pear tree broken by the storm.*
>
> *I count those feathered balls of soot*
> *The moorhen guides upon the stream,*
> *To silence the envy in my thought;*
> *And turn towards my chamber, caught*
> *In the cold snow of a dream.*

The sense of discouragement, and the dream image that always accompanies in Yeats a temporary questioning of endeavour, is extremely moving. The choice is made, and it seems more than a temporary one; the Mask appears to be laid aside for a moment and the real Yeats to appear, subject to an envy and dejection in which any of his readers can share. But this is not really the case. 'The real Yeats' is a misleading phrase, for the appearance of hesitation is itself a Mask, a kind of behaviour that has been meticulously

studied in the genesis of the poem. What we can observe is
how completely Yeats has turned the experience to his own
account: the study of his own possibilities of behaviour is the
real *donnée* of the fact of civil war, which is seen in terms of
natural disturbance—the pear tree broken by the storm—a
method of imaging which connects with his other apprehensions of nature. Sometimes the life of action that he sees
himself as renouncing is a pastoral one, the sporting routine
of the country gentleman, but, like all activity in Yeats, the
style makes it seem as stark and heroic as war itself.

> *I leave both faith and pride*
> *To young upstanding men*
> *Climbing the mountain side*
> *That under bursting dawn*
> *They may drop a fly,*
> *Being of that metal made*
> *Till it was broken by*
> *This sedentary trade.*
>
> (*The Tower*)

If it were not married so closely to the Masks, the new style
would be at times a little too inflexible, even cumbrous: its
abrupt simplicity implies a corresponding harshness of feeling, and feeling might be controlled too strictly by the kind
of words that Yeats likes to use. But as it is, 'the confusion of
the death bed', 'the delirium of the brave', take their place
beside the life of the country gentleman in the orderly and
yet passionate arrangement of Yeats's experience.

One of the assumptions of the Mask is that poetry and life
are indivisible, that ways of behaving in life are the same as
ways of writing in poetry, and that therefore art may and
should have a deep effect on action. Yeats is constantly echoing the Romantic idea first voiced by Shelley; 'the laws of

Art are the hidden laws of the world', and he writes in *Ideas of Good and Evil*, 'I am never certain, when I hear of some war, or some religious excitement, or of some new manufacture, or of anything else that fills the ear of the world, that it has not all happened because of something a boy piped in Thessaly.' The reader may smile at this, but Yeats is deadly serious. After the Irish riots on Queen Victoria's jubilee he writes: 'I count the links in the chain of responsibility, and wonder if there is any from my workshop.' One of his last poems repeats the problem.

> *All that I have said and done,*
> *Now that I am old and ill,*
> *Turns into a question till*
> *I lie awake night after night*
> *And never get the answers right.*
> *Did that play of mine send out*
> *Certain men the English shot?*
>
> (*The Man and the Echo*)

Yeats is certainly the last Romantic to believe implicitly in the power of poetry, whether he believed in the power of magic or not. As we shall see, though Auden has learnt from Yeats to create a world of his own, he does not believe—as Yeats believed—that this world either can have or should have power to change men's actions or to 'legislate' to the real world. It is difficult for us not to feel a certain incredulity at Yeats's distress about the effect his words may have had, but there is no doubt that the distress is genuine, and it shows how great and how poetically valuable was his self-confidence. The Mask of the conscience-stricken poet is not absurd when Yeats wears it.

Since the source of all poetry is human behaviour and the 'quarrel with ourselves' that enables the poet to display its passion and variety, it follows that all value in the world comes from human endeavour and from that alone.

> *Whatever flames upon the night*
> *Man's own resinous heart has fed.*

This, the final conclusion to which his meditation on a Mask leads him, is emphasised again and again by Yeats. 'Men will no longer separate the idea of God from the idea of human genius, human productivity in all its forms.' This conviction prompts some of his most graphic poetic statements. 'Man has created death'—

> *Though grave-diggers' toil is long,*
> *Sharp their spades, their muscles strong,*
> *They but thrust their buried men*
> *Back in the human mind again.*
>
> (*Under Ben Bulben*)

The philosophers whom he has studied and made use of are at fault.

> *I mock Plotinus' thought*
> *And cry in Plato's teeth*
> *That life and death were not*
> *Till man made up the whole,*
> *Made lock, stock, and barrel*
> *Out of his bitter soul.*

The 'self-begotten soul'

> *—learns at last that it is self-delighting,*
> *Self-appeasing, self-affrighting,*
> *And that its own sweet will is heaven's will. . . .*

It learns, too, that 'natural and supernatural with the self-same ring are wed'. So impressed was Yeats with this truth to which meditation had led him that he set an inordinate value upon poems by W. J. Turner and Dorothy Wellesley in which he detected the same cherished belief. We can see from this both how much Yeats could value an 'idea', a poem's prose kernel, for its own sake, and how masterfully he could himself ring the changes upon such an *idée fixe* in his own poetry. It reveals at a deeper level, moreover, how irrelevant is the question, often critically discussed, of whether Yeats's theories and experiments in magic do not vitiate his whole poetic outlook. Critics have maintained, for example, that *All Souls' Night* is spoilt by being a 'magical' poem. In fact, so self-contained is Yeats's universe, so determined by his passionate interest in human endeavour, sex, and death (the only topics, as he remarks in a letter, 'of interest to a serious and studious mind'), that his interest in magic subordinates itself naturally inside this context. He would have thought the word 'supernatural' as question-begging as it would be to a logical positivist, or to a scientist who might admit the existence of physical phenomena which had not yet been explained.

If the final theoretical position of the Mask is man 'self-sufficing and eternal', complete in every one of his moods and appearances, its final display is the Mask of irreverence, the wisdom of the Fool. This attitude, which had always been implicit in Yeats's programme of traditional poses—'lover, sage, hero, scorner of life'—becomes increasingly his favourite in his last poems. With it he derided the other attitudes, the symbols and abstract ideas of his maturity.

> *My circus animals were all on show,*
> *Those stilted boys, that burnished chariot,*
> *Lion and woman and the Lord knows what.*

But they survive the derision, for the irreverent gibe is no final 'position of wisdom', but itself only a Mask. Yeats had foreshadowed his late Mask much earlier, as early as 1904, when one of his best plays, *On Baile's Strand*, was first acted. In it are contrasted the wise king Conchobar and the gay hero Cuchulain, but there are also the blind man and the Fool, and after Cuchulain has rushed out to fight the waves, this couple are left in the house.

> FOOL: He has killed kings and giants, but the waves have mastered him, the waves have mastered him!
> BLIND MAN: Come here, Fool!
> FOOL: The waves have mastered him.
> BLIND MAN: Come here!
> FOOL: The waves have mastered him.
> BLIND MAN: Come here, I say.
> FOOL: What is it?
> BLIND MAN: There will be nobody in the houses. Come this way; come quickly! The ovens will be full. We will put our hands into the ovens.

In the spare and scurrilous poems of his old age Yeats consciously invites a certain ambivalence in the reader's attitude. 'Read it as either the hidden meaning of the Sage, or Sing a Song of Sixpence.' Earnestness was one Mask he would not employ, for 'wisdom is a butterfly and not a gloomy bird of prey'. To be mysterious was in order, but not to be heavy and persuasive. 'People', Yeats remarks in his survey of modern poetry in the preface to the *Oxford Book of Modern Verse*, 'began to imitate old ballads, because an old ballad is never rhetorical. I think of *The Shropshire Lad*, of certain poems by Hardy, of Kipling's *St Helena Lullaby* and of his *Looking Glass*.' Since so much of his own poetry might be called rhetorical, we may be puzzled by Yeats's dislike of the idea of rhetoric, until we remember that Verlaine's *Art Poétique*, with its line,

> *Prends l'éloquence et tords-lui son cou,*

had been all the rage in Yeats's youth, and that *l'éloquence* was the vice of persuasiveness and emotional facility associated with Hugo and his imitators. The avoidance of such defects, behind whom hovered his old *bête noire* of 'sincerity', was one of the principal aims of the Masks. Ballads and their refrains came to seem to him one of the best ways of illustrating the 'truths and counter-truths' of the Mask. He greatly admired *The Pretty Maid*, a ballad adapted from the French of Paul Fort by York Powell, who was, like Housman, a noted academic figure, Regius Professor of History at Oxford.

> *The pretty maid, she died, she died; in love-bed as she lay.*
> *They bore her to the churchyard, all at the break of day.*
> *They left her all alone there: all in her white array;*
> *They left her all alone there: a'coffined in the clay.*
> *And they marched back so merrily, all at the dawn of day;*
> *A'singing all so merrily: 'The dog must have his day'.*
> *The pretty maid is dead, is dead; in love-bed as she lay,*
> *And they are off afield to work, as they do every day.*

York Powell's academic satisfaction in this robust attitude arose no doubt from its similarity to Homer. Aldous Huxley, in a well-known essay, has called it 'telling the whole truth', and has given as an example the scene in the *Odyssey* where the sailors who have escaped from the jaws of Scylla prepare their supper first before lamenting the death of their comrades. Huxley, and other critics who have admired this classical honesty, have opposed it by implication to the simplified and exaggerated emotions of romanticism. Yeats adds to the confusion by announcing that 'Homer is my example, and his unchristened heart'. But—as so often in Yeats—imitation, example, are the key words. By means of the Mask or the ballad, he and York Powell are contriving a piece of 'whole truth' with such sophisticated deliberation that any reference to Homer, or classical dispassion, seems beside the point. Aware of the dangers of romantic 'eloquence', Yeats is simply making use of a 'classical' model to enlarge his romantic universe. *'The dog must have his day'* might well be one of his own ballad refrains, like *Daybreak and a candle-end* or *The Colonel went out sailing*, intended, by their homely repetitive incongruity, to disrupt some elevated argument and recall the poet to a 'counter-truth'.

> *All men live in suffering,*
> *I know as few can know,*
> *Whether they take the upper road*
> *Or stay content on the low,*
> *Rower bent in his row-boat*
> *Or weaver bent at his loom,*
> *Horsemen erect upon horseback*
> *Or child hid in the womb.*
> > *Daybreak and a candle-end.*
>
> *That some stream of lightning*
> *From the old man in the skies*
> *Can burn out that suffering*
> *No right-taught man denies.*
> *But a coarse old man am I,*
> *I choose the second-best,*
> *I forget it all awhile*
> *Upon a woman's breast.*
> > *Daybreak and a candle-end.*
> > > (*The Wild Old Wicked Man*)

Sometimes, as in *The Statesman's Holiday*, it is the 'theme' itself which is scurrilous and the refrain of a heraldic magnificence. *Tall dames go walking in grass-green Avalon.*

Yeats's poetry of conversation has carried this *genre* to a point which is unlikely to be surpassed, and since our purpose is to show how he made use of and added new life to the romantic tradition, we must examine his methods here. For conversational poetry appealed to the early Romantics by reason of its element of spontaneity, of the possibilities it offered for theorising or for exploring a state of mind. But whereas the conversational poetry of the eighteenth century is social in tone—the poet seeming to address his friends and patrons, a closed circle on whose attention he could rely—that of the nineteenth is a monologue, a voice uncertain of its audience and often in consequence rambling like a sleep-talker, rising to hysteria or sinking into an interminable mutter—the voice of a man who knows he is alone. Browning, Tennyson, Patmore, all wrote poetry of this kind—talkative in tone, but as impersonal as Meredith's conversation, which had begun before a visitor's arrival and continued after he left. It expounds a system or airs a prejudice without consideration for the boredom of the audience. Now Yeats, as we know, had a system, and in many of his intermediate poems he deploys it—often in dialogue form—with this Victorian thoroughness. *Shepherd and Goatherd, Ego Dominus Tuus* (which Ezra Pound used irreverently to call Hic and Willie), and *The Phases of the Moon* are such poems. Here is an extract from the last.

ROBARTES: *Twenty-and-eight the phases of the moon,*
The full and the moon's dark and all the crescents,
Twenty-and-eight, and yet but six-and-twenty
The cradles that a man must needs be rocked in:
For there's no human life at the full or the dark.

From the first crescent to the half, the dream
But summons to adventure and the man
Is always happy like a bird or beast;
But while the moon is rounding towards the full
He follows whatever whim's most difficult. . . .

and so on. Here is the system which Yeats expounded fully in *A Vision*, the human attitudes allotted in the moon's phases, the planetary cones, the interpenetrating gyres of reason and emotion, and all the rest of it. And when expounded in poetry they have a certain geometric fascination, but they are also liable to bewilder and bore the reader. Yeats came to realise this perfectly well. He describes how the spirits who brought him the material of *A Vision* declined his offer to spend the rest of his life in interpreting their messages, and announced that they had come to bring him 'metaphors for poetry'. Henceforth he brings in his theories in poems, not as if he were addressing an audience, but as if he were talking with friends about something with which they were already familiar. He refers rather than explains: and he can also suddenly throw the whole thing overboard with a gesture and speak in a different key and to a different purpose. The Mask and 'counter-truth' affected him here, but so did his theory of what conversation should be like—brilliant, variable, inconsistent, assuming the possession by the speakers of a common background of knowledge and taste: an eighteenth-century idea, in fact. His father had remarked in a letter that a drugged cigar should be kept for any conversationalist 'who pointed out that one had just said something quite inconsistent with what one had said before'. We may be sure that Yeats agreed. He came to assume in the circle of his readers some knowledge of his ideas and some acceptance of their vagaries, just as in his last poems he assumes their acquaintance with the thinkers who interest him. Thus he writes in *A Bronze Head* (the subject is his memory of Maud Gonne)—

> *No dark tomb-haunter once; her form all full*
> *As though with magnanimity of light,*
> *Yet a most gentle woman; who can tell*
> *Which of her forms has shown her substance right:*
> *Or maybe substance can be composite,*
> *Profound MacTaggart thought so, and in a breath*
> *A mouthful held the extreme of life and death.*

Profound MacTaggart lends both weight and ease to the stanza. His appearance and his reported views (what we can catch of them) are impressive, but we do not have to know that he was a Cambridge philosopher with a theory of Time in whom Yeats was interested. We gather it, as we might gather and profit from the *ambiance* of a conversation in which some great names, easily produced, are strange to us. This is the very height of conversation, and the verse reproduces the tone of it with an almost uncanny accuracy. The question, the hesitation—that 'Or maybe'—and the authority abruptly produced, with a lift of the eyebrows or thrust of the forefinger. How Yeats can combine this excited and yet urbane distinction of talk with the full, unselfconscious nobility of the description, and fit its rolling polysyllables—*tomb-haunter, magnanimity*—into his colloquially free pentameter line, is a miracle of which he alone had the secret.

One of his most telling conversational devices is an affected change of mind, or correction of some point previously made.

> *Strange, but the man who made the song was blind,*
> *But now I have considered it I find*
> *That nothing strange . . .*

The Statues opens with a vigorous statement and question.

> *Pythagoras planned it. Why did the people stare?*

But at the beginning of the second stanza, Yeats, with an equal vigour, changes his mind.

> *No! Greater than Pythagoras, for the men*
> *That with a mallet or a chisel modelled these*
> *Calculations that look but casual flesh, put down*
> *All Asiatic vague immensities . . .*

Sometimes the vigour of speech is achieved by a repetition—

> *I dream of a Ledaean body, bent*
> *Above a sinking fire, a tale that she*
> *Told of a harsh reproof, or trivial event*
> *That changed some childish day to tragedy—*
> *Told, and it seemed that our two natures blent*
> *Into a sphere from youthful sympathy . . .*
>
> *(Among School-Children)*

It is in these ways that Yeats combines an offhand occasional manner with the impression that

> *A passion-driven exultant man sings out*
> *Sentences that he has never thought—*

and to give his verse energy he needs rhyme, with its gift of 'a natural momentum of syntax', as a runner needs oxygen. With blank verse he is never happy, as the plays and the blank verse poems referred to, like *The Phases of the Moon*, show. Since Shakespeare, blank verse has never been successfully employed with the variety, passion, and colloquial vigour that Yeats sought for, and though he learnt much from Shakespeare's and Donne's ability to shorten or elongate the decasyllabic line, he can only use it successfully in a rhyming stanza. Blank verse forces on him an expository anonymous tone; *Among School-Children* and *The Statues* are to the blank verse poems what Keats's odes are to his *Hyperion*: the blank verse produces in both poets a style that is dignified and hieratic, but composite, unindividualised, and finally inert. Curiously enough there are even verbal resemblances to *Hyperion* in *The Phases of the Moon*—

> *Athene takes Achilles by the hair* . . .

is very close to Keats's

> *She might have ta'en*
> *Achilles by the hair and bent his neck*
> *Or with a finger stayed Ixion's wheel* . . .

and in both cases the verse tradition of Marlowe-Miltonic weight has sapped the poet's individuality. But in the rhymed pentameter poems we can detect traditional influence at its best—as inspiration rather than as handicap. If we compare *A Bronze Head*, in particular, with certain speeches in *King Lear* or *The Winter's Tale*, we can see what admirable use, both in verse movement and vocabulary, Yeats made of his constant reading of Shakespeare. Although, unlike Robert Bridges, he never took any interest in metrical analysis and theory, Yeats had a remarkable natural ear for effects just 'off the beat' of the decasyllable. He was pleased when Bridges congratulated him for producing in *The Wanderings of Oisin* a line movement that 'had never been known in English verse before'—

> *Fled foam underneath us, and round us, a wandering and*
> *milky smoke*—

and the verse innovations of his maturity can often be traced to a cunning overloading of unstressed or half-stressed syllables in the second half of a line.

> *Told of a harsh reproof or trivial event . . .*
> *Through three enchanted islands, allegorical dreams . . .*
> *Profound MacTaggart thought so, and in a breath . . .*

As in the Metaphysicals, it is the mundane speech pattern, with its afterthoughts and breakings-off, that keeps the logical thread in these poems running so clearly. This logical structure, or the effect of it, was much valued by Yeats. 'Though much of it is powerful and musical', he wrote of Swinburne's *Faustina*, 'it could not be understood with pleasure because it has no more logical structure than a bag of shot.' How he could impress an internal logic on a poem without recourse either to a descriptive or symbolic 'plot' or to the tedium of argument and exposition is well shown by *A Dialogue of Self and Soul*. Dialogue poems, as 'Hic and Willie' shows, are not usually Yeats's strong point. But this poem is a dialogue only in name: in fact it is a measured, alternating soliloquy. Except for a brief moment in the third stanza, neither Soul nor Body pays any attention to what the other is saying. Both seem rather to be conversing with a circle of friends, perhaps the same friends whose ghostly presences are summoned up in *All Souls' Night*. And what might have been an intellectual dispute is prevented by the romantic gestures that each makes to its audience. First, the Self, with 'Sato's ancient blade' upon his knees, asserts his unquenched sensuous vitality (Yeats was very ill when he wrote the poem in 1928). Between whiles the Soul, taking the darkness of the Tower as his emblem, identifies himself with silence and extinction—'Who can distinguish darkness from the soul?'

Think of ancestral night that can
If but imagination scorn the earth
And intellect its wandering
To this and that and t'other thing,
Deliver from the crime of death and birth.

A verse of Self follows, but the Soul's argument goes straight on without heeding it.

Such fullness in that quarter overflows
And falls into the basin of the mind
That man is stricken deaf and dumb and blind,
For intellect no longer knows
Is from the Ought, or Knower from the Known . . .

'*Is* from the *Ought*, or *Knower* from the *Known*'—the Soul has reached the dry bones of Yeats's dialectic—*What is*, which is the *Will*: *What ought to be*, which is the *Mask*: the *Knower*, who is the *Creative Mind*: and the *Known*, or *Body of Fate*. These, corresponding to the quarters of the moon, are the four determinants of the individual's life on earth.

But the Soul's part in the dialogue is now over, and before the reader has time to be checked or puzzled by this cryptic saying, which could hardly be explained except by reference to material outside the poem itself, and which Yeats quickly brushes aside with the bald explanation,

That is to say, ascends to Heaven

the Self has taken over for good, and the great peroration has begun.

A living man is blind and drinks his drop.
What matter if the ditches are impure?
What matter if I live it all once more?

The tremendous gesture of assent is not determined by what has gone before. Yeats does not reach a conclusion: he cuts the poem short in the most effective way. None the less, the structure of the poem, the contrast between the acquiescence in darkness and the enduring thirst for life, is graphically maintained, assisted by the emblems of life and death, the sword and the tower, and by the great rhetoric of assent which brings the poem to its climax. But though it has its hard core of 'subject' and develops in conformity to it, there is nothing considered, nothing judicial and well-weighed about the poem. Despite his labour and revision and his care for logic, Yeats detested poetry that bore an air of finality, of ultimate *arrival*. Though in most ways so different from T. S. Eliot, he would have echoed the latter's pronouncement that 'every attempt' in poetry 'is a wholly new start'. It was for this reason that he disliked Valéry's *Cimetière Marin*, whose subject is curiously similar to that of *A Dialogue of Self and Soul*. Both poets feel that the painful and ignorant process of living minute by minute is better than a state of empty tranquillity and comprehension. 'A living man is blind and drinks his drop'—*Le vent se lève, il faut tenter de vivre*. Valéry's conclusion is calm, unemotional, a deprecating shrug of the shoulders: Yeats's outburst is a passionate slogan to keep his courage up and to assert the appearance of poetic vitality— 'What matter?' is a charm which can resolve every situation and liberate him from every dilemma. 'What matter if the ditches are impure?'—'What matter if numb nightmare ride on top / And blood and mire the sensitive body stain?'— 'What matter if there are scores beside? / I knew a phoenix in my youth so let them have their day.' There is a danger, often present, that gay defiance will become *ipso facto* poetic for Yeats, as stoicism was for Housman.

The troubles of our proud and angry dust
Are from eternity, and shall not fail.
Bear them we can, and if we can we must.

Yeats's versatile power, his 'intellectual receptivity', and his great strength in poetic co-ordination, need not hide the similarity of his romantic impulse to which he returns after all his richness of speculation and contradiction. He must have something to fall back on, after each new departure has been made, and the end of his poem is not a conclusion, like Valéry's, but—like Housman's—a grand dismissive gesture.

The use of the word 'emblem' in *A Dialogue of Self and Soul* brings us to the last and perhaps most important of Yeats's developments of the romantic and Symbolist tradition. His increasing fondness, in his later poetry, for the term 'emblem' as opposed to 'symbol' has a particular significance. It implies an image method more limited, more clear-cut, more down to earth in every way than the deliberate vagueness of effect which was aimed at by the Symbolist poets. It reminds us, in fact, of the Emblem Books of the sixteenth and seventeenth centuries, where each emblem had its straightforward allegorical gloss. Yeats's Tower and Sword, 'the Lion and the Virgin, the Harlot and the Child' —'the circus animals' as he once called them—are all emblems of this kind. And, as we have seen in *A Dialogue*, they are employed, mingled with passion and conversation, to illustrate a logical theme, much as Valéry illustrates his theme in *Le Cimetière Marin* (though Yeats would not have cared for the comparison) with the movement of the white sails on the sea and the stillness of the white graves in the churchyard. Such an employment is clear and orderly, and it is in no adverse sense that we refer to it as 'illustration'. On the contrary, the emblems are carefully chosen for their exact correlation to the theme, for their pictorial beauty (a fried egg would not be a good *emblem*, however relevant to the poet's thought, though it might be effectively used as an *image*)—and most important of all, for their docility: they will not, like vaguer or more complex symbols and metaphors, spill out into the poem and blur its theme with a life of their own.

For Yeats was acutely aware of the Symbolists' dilemma: how to retain 'the indefiniteness of music' in addition to *meaning* something; or, alternatively, how to present a definite Symbol—Maeterlinck's 'blue bird', for example—without the risk of its being brutally allegorised by an insensitive public. As soon as Symbolism becomes a conscious policy of the artist it runs the risk of becoming allegory. Hence the admission of Arthur Symons, one of the interpreters of the movement, that symbolism has always and necessarily been used by poets, whether they knew what they were doing or not; and hence the reluctance of the Symbolist poets who *did* know what they were doing to be anything but mysterious and evasive. They seem banded in a slightly absurd conspiracy, as if they were saying: 'We know why we are doing this, but we do not know what we mean by it and could not afford to say so if we did.' Involuntarily the technique invited an interpretation, but its exponents were pained if one were made. French Symbolism derived very largely from Poe, and from one poem of his in particular—*The Haunted Palace*—in which the palace symbolises a young man who goes mad. This signification is not of course explicitly stated, but the detail leaves us in no doubt. As Housman comments, by the time we read—

> *Along the ramparts plumed and pallid*
> *A winged odour went away*

—we can only attempt to avert our minds from the knowledge that this is a symbol for the young man's hair-oil. Poe, to do him justice, would no doubt have welcomed an awareness of the connection—his view of the matter was as robust as that of a mediaeval allegorist, though his ideas on 'suggestiveness' vetoed the appending of an actual *significacio*. But his French admirers had no trouble in averting their minds. And so we reach the Symbolist *impasse* in which the two girls in Mallarmé's *L'Après-Midi d'un Faune*, for example, quite obviously *represent* water and sun, and yet this fact is only permitted to reach the reader's sensibility as a 'suggestion'. Such symbolism can only be talked about, can only be apprehended in fact, in terms of allegory.

It was this situation that Yeats had somehow to resolve. As a young man he simply accepted it. G. M. Hopkins mentions in a letter one of Yeats's very early, very symbolic, and unpublished poems which described a young man and a sphinx alone on a rock in the middle of the sea, and comments: 'How did they get there? What did they eat? etc. People think such criticism very prosaic but commonsense is never out of place anywhere.' An elaborately symbolic pattern does indeed invite this sort of response, and Yeats soon took refuge in the faery vagueness of *The Wanderings of Oisin*, where the symbols of earthly endeavour—'vain gaiety, vain battle, vain repose'—as he later described the poem—are so diluted and uninsistent that we hardly notice them. But the new style and the Mask theory also changed his ideas about the handling of the symbol. As early as 1900 he was writing of symbols that 'evoke emotion alone', and 'intellectual ones that evoke ideas alone'. In this idea of an intellectual symbol the concept of the Emblem seems already discernible. 'If I say *white* or *purple* in an ordinary line of poetry', he goes on, 'they evoke emotions so exclusively that

I cannot say why they move me, but if I say them in the same breath with such obviously intellectual symbols as a cross or a crown of thorns, I think of purity or sovereignty.' This certainly foreshadows the poetry of a much later date.

> *A storm-beaten old watch-tower,*
> *A blind hermit rings the hour.*

> *All-destroying sword-blade still*
> *Carried by the wandering fool.*

> *Gold-sewn silk on the sword-blade,*
> *Beauty and fool together laid.*
> <div align="right">(<i>Symbols</i>)</div>

and,

> *The sword's a cross; thereon He died:*
> *On breast of Mars the goddess sighed.*

He had come to realise that nothing can be so effectively mysterious as precision, and a hard image that—even if it is cryptic—sets the intellect at work.

In the early criticism the distinction between intellect and emotion is crude, and Yeats very properly hastens to blur it over with long Paterian sentences. What appealed to him most at the time, it is interesting to notice, was the possibility offered by Symbolist theory of creating a mirror world, in which the poet's materials would be reflected, transformed by his symbolic self, instead of being offered baldly to the reader in their own right. The changes that the theory will bring to poetry, he forecasts, 'will be a casting out of descriptions of nature for the sake of nature, of the moral law for the sake of the moral law, a casting out of all anecdotes and of all that brooding over scientific opinion

that so often extinguished the central flame in Tennyson, and
of that vehemence which would make us do or not do certain things'. In the light of Yeats's later poetry this may
strike us as odd. Anecdotes, brooding over scientific opinion,
and a vehemence which could lead to distress over the consequences it may have had on men's actions, is precisely
what distinguishes his poetic maturity. But the atmosphere
of Symbolism has done its work; still making use of his early
perception of its value to him, and enclosed in its 'superhuman, mirror-resembling dream', he can brood, tell
stories, and be as vehement as he likes.

None the less, Poe's Haunted Palace and the young man
and the sphinx who amused Hopkins are not entirely
banished, even after the success of the emblems. Many of the
critical differences about and attacks on the *Byzantium* poems
arise from the too great rigidity of their symbolic structure.
There is a tendency to try and fit all the details into a pattern
of meaning, and this—as in cruder symbolist poems—can
shrink the legend's magnificence into the merely banal. Thus
William Empson, on the strength of the first line of
Byzantium—

The unpurged images of day recede;

—comments that 'Yeats gets there [to Byzantium] and finds
an ordinary type of fascist state, gross, brutal, and violent.
The memories of what he saw there during the day have to
fade before his vision of ghostly and eternal perfection—the
thing he came there to see—can arise again in his mind.' This
is surely to press the symbolic correlation too far, though it
is true that the machinery of the poem does unfortunately
encourage such probing. Empson's supposition of a political
flavour, and the attack on Yeats for his preference in the
poem for a barbarous and autocratic, though art-loving

society, are, in a sense, criticisms of the poem in spite of their irrelevance, because they show that Yeats has not succeeded in achieving that absolute, self-contained poem world which he most valued. *Byzantium* relies rather too much on its poised speed and virtuosity, a speed that carries the reader over the jagged edges of the fable, and its tone—unlike the calm of *Sailing to Byzantium*—is one of controlled frenzy; it is a *breathless* poem, breathless in the same sense as the mouths which summon the spirits in the second stanza—

> *A mouth that has no moisture and no breath*
> *Breathless mouths may summon. . . .*

The word here is indicative of the poem's verbal quality, which is hurried, less meticulously grand than we expect from Yeats. It is significant that he first wrote *breathing mouths*, a good sense contrast with the breathless mouths of the dead, and changed it in the interest of sound and because it increased the poem's generalised effect. The substitution of course still makes sense, but is less contextually apt, and creates—like certain other phrases,—*embittered, complexities of fury* reversed into *furies of complexity*—a blur in the pattern of coherence. The images of the last stanza—

> *. . . The smithies break the flood,*
> *The golden smithies of the Emperor!*
> *Marbles of the dancing floor*
> *Break bitter furies of complexity—*

are decidedly clumsy and uncomfortable if we have time to reflect on them. They are in fact mixed metaphors, and in a bad sense, because they are confusing the verbal picture which they are intended to build. Yeats has fallen for once into the old Symbolist snare. The smithies 'breaking the flood', and the dancing floor breaking the 'furies of complexity', appeal to their abstract purport in the general myth of the poem, without being natural, on the first level, as elementary action. They mean something at the expense of their existence as images, not by virtue of it.

What they do mean—the triumph of order, harmony, and artificial grace among the shadowy hurly-burly of man's desires and experiences, 'the fury and the mire of human veins'—was first conceived of by Yeats as an emblem, the artificial gold song-bird of the Emperor. From this emblem and its meaning for him—the marvellous and eternal artifice which he opposes to the world of nature—the rest of the symbolic structure of Byzantium followed, but we may feel that it is the single emblem itself, and what Yeats understood by it, that gives impressiveness to the poems and makes *Sailing to Byzantium* by far the more impressive of the two. For the earlier poem has a much simpler symbolic structure than the later; it mingles its emblematic motif with statement and homely idiom—

> *An aged man is but a paltry thing*
> *A tattered cloak upon a stick . . .*

and it begins with admirable abruptness—'That is no country for old men.' As the stanza proceeds we learn that Yeats is speaking of the realm of nature, the country of the young, and we are spared the remorselessly sequential development which a symbolic poem often unrolls. The early drafts of the poem show that Yeats did begin with this chronological scheme, starting in the country of the young and progressing by easy stages, as it were, to Byzantium.

> *I therefore travel to Byzantium*
> *Among those sun-brown pleasant mariners,*
> *Another dozen days and we shall come*
> *Under the jetty and the marble stairs. . . .*

The effect of a leisurely cruise is obviously incongruous, and the final version successfully jumps the intermediate steps.

The shifting from one self-contained emblem to another, with a conversational *armature* in between, is Yeats's final and best solution to the Symbolist problem—what he seems to have meant by 'articulating the images'. Not that he ever finally abandoned the organic method: *The Black Tower*, one of his last poems, imagines a garrison awaiting the return of their chief, some enigmatic power in whose survival they obstinately continue to believe. But the detail is naturalistic, not symbolic; we may be sure that

> *The tower's old cook that must climb and clamber*
> *Catching small birds in the dew of the morn—*

has no recondite significance, but is simply a delightful and moving detail of the legend. In *Meru* there is a similar combination of reality and personal symbol. Yeats begins the poem with one of his characteristic reflections.

> *Civilisation is hooped together, brought*
> *Under a rule, under the semblance of peace*
> *By manifold illusion; but man's life is thought.* . . .

The first stanza develops this historical vision; then comes the key line,

> *Hermits upon Mount Meru or Everest,*

The cycle of man 'ravening through century after century' is stilled, and the abstract tempo of the poem halted into a cold image of contemplation—the movement of the line, with its strong extra syllable *Mount*, intensifies the change. Coupled with the associations of Everest, Meru sounds like a real mountain, but it is in fact another name for *Abiegnos*, the sacred mount in the mythology of a theosophic group

called The Golden Dawn, in which Yeats had been a leading
spirit. In his mixed mythology the real and the imaginary
are juxtaposed with complete assurance, for both achieve an
equal mythological status by the fact of his use of them. It is
the same in *The Statues*.

> *When Pearse summoned Cuchulain to his side*
> *What stalked through the Post Office?*

And his own life, his own disappointments and emotional
failures, his hatred of growing old, can be all turned into
mythology in one long and marvellous sentence.

> *Now shall I make my soul,*
> *Compelling it to study*
> *In a learned school*
> *Till the wreck of body,*
> *Slow decay of blood,*
> *Testy delirium*
> *Or dull decrepitude,*
> *Or what worse evil come—*
> *The death of friends, or death*
> *Of every brilliant eye*
> *That made a catch in the breath—*
> *Seem but the clouds in the sky*
> *When the horizon fades;*
> *Or a bird's sleepy cry*
> *Among the deepening shades.*

Yeats's greatness can finally be measured by his determination to survive as a poet—and as the same sort of poet—
no matter what changes of attitude the progress of his life
seemed to require of him. Far from displaying in his later
years that 'leaden acquiescence in defeat' which Edmund
Wilson professed to detect, he continued to show how all

the old romantic properties, the symbols and the attitudes, could survive triumphantly in the modern world, asserting themselves with an extraordinary completeness and vigour against the contemporary background of hesitancy, lack of confidence, or strategic withdrawal to traditional beliefs. About his contemporary, the poet John Davidson, he remarked in the *Autobiographies*: 'He lacked intellectual receptivity, lacked pose and gesture, and now no verse of his clings to my memory.' These are the precise qualities—and memorability above all—which Yeats's verse has, the qualities which he valued supremely in poetry and which he was himself so concerned to possess.

CHAPTER IX

W. H. Auden

YEATS'S POETIC statements often end, as we have seen, on a note of acceptance—acceptance of everything that life has to offer. But when we compare it with other kinds of literary expression we may feel that this attitude is one that goes well into poetry but bears little relation to the lives we actually have to lead.

> *Irrational streams of blood are staining earth;*
> *Empedocles has thrown all things about;*
> *Hector is dead and there's a light in Troy;*
> *We that look on but laugh in tragic joy.*
>
> (*The Gyres*)

The effect of incantation is obvious and superb. The identity of Empedocles, and why his influence should have been so unsettling, remain unimportant. The forces that threaten to destroy us are of an august kind, Yeats seems to be saying, and we should have enough sense of style to find that consoling. None the less, it is a long way from the world of Hector to the world of Hitler; we are not Housman's 'Spartans on the sea-wet rock', and we are not the tragic heroes and heroines whom Yeats invokes as models of decorum when times are bad.

All perform their tragic play,
There struts Hamlet, there is Lear,
That's Ophelia, that Cordelia;
Yet they, should the last scene be there,
The great stage curtain about to drop,
If worthy their prominent part in the play,
Do not break up their lines to weep.
They know that Hamlet and Lear are gay.

(*Lapis Lazuli*)

Our individual lives, in the midst of the twentieth century, do not seem much related to this. They are complex, difficult, random, perhaps horrifying, certainly concerned with issues which appear to demand some other response than tragic gaiety. Yeats's 'acceptance' of life, in fact, often seems very much like a renunciation—where poetry is concerned —of what actually happens in life.

Whose poetry should we expect to grapple with these problems, and produce in us the attitudes which, in I. A. Richards's idiom, will be of value to us in our actual world and enable us to live effectively in it? Surely that of W. H. Auden. At the time of Yeats's final phase, Auden belonged to a group of poets whose aims were intimately connected with social and political questions; he was learned in psychology and anthropology; his approach was avowedly 'scientific'—that is to say, detailed, enquiring, impartial; he believed that an artist should be 'more than a bit of a reporting journalist'; he was in touch with all the latest ideas and the latest developments. Apparently, his whole approach to life and art could scarcely have been more different from that of Yeats. And yet as we read his poetry, and in particular the early volumes, we feel that the response we give them— and the response they appear to require—is not so different.

Not that Auden renounces by implication what actually happens in most people's lives: on the contrary he is passionately interested in all the details. But the mechanism by which his poetry bites on to such material—rhetorical, self-confident to the point of arrogance, intent on securing the advantage of an immediate effect—all this is very like Yeats.

Get there if you can and see the land you once were proud to own
Though the roads have almost vanished and the expresses never
*   run:*

Smokeless chimneys, damaged bridges, rotting wharves and choked
*   canals,*
Tramlines buckled, smashed trucks lying on their side across the
*   rails;*

Power-stations locked, deserted, since they drew the boiler fires,
Pylons falling or subsiding, trailing dead high-tension wires;

Head-gears gaunt on grass-grown pitbanks, seams abandoned years
*   ago;*
Drop a stone and listen for its splash in flooded dark below. . . .

These were boon companions who devised the legends for our
*   tombs,*
These who have betrayed us nicely while we took them to our
*   rooms.*

Newman, Ciddy, Plato, Fronny, Pascal, Bowdler, Baudelaire,
Doctor Frommer, Mrs Allan, Freud, the Baron, and Flaubert,

Lured with their compelling logic, charmed with beauty of their
*   verse,*
With their loaded sideboards whispered, 'Better join us, life is
*   worse'. . . .*

On the sopping esplanade or from our dingy lodgings we
Stare out dully at the rain which falls for miles into the sea.

(*Poems,* 1930. No. 22)

The gusto and sense of enjoyment here is extraordinary. As in Yeats, violence and calamity are on the way: the signs of their coming—industrial chaos, bourgeois artiness and escapism, cramped and wasted lives—are graphically described, with a pungency and detail of which Auden is already a complete master in his first 1930 volume. He has taken the metre of *Locksley Hall,* the use of which for full-blooded egotistic declamation was one of Tennyson's greatest discoveries, and he handles it with characteristic skill. He shares with Yeats an enjoyment of the situation and of the possibilities of making it *stylish.* The picture of desolation gives the reader a thrill of gratified excitement: he seems to be sharing in a vicarious *Schadenfreude,* and indulging too in the thoughtless pleasures of youth, like dropping the stone down the old working and waiting for the splash. Even the esplanade, and the hilarious precision of *sopping* and *dingy,* only give the reader that retrospective warmth which comes from remembering the boredom and glamour of childhood holidays. Staring out dully at the rain evokes at once all the rich futility of nostalgic recollection. Everything is hopeless and the country is going to the dogs, but to think this, while staring out at the rain, is somehow no inconsiderable pleasure. The attitude gives us, in some obscure way, a sense of mastery. 'Man has the refuge of his gaiety.' Or the refuge, at least, of a purely personal reaction. The tradition goes back much further. There is the silence of Don Juan in hell which Baudelaire admired—

> *Mais le calme héros, courbé sur sa rapière,*
> *Regardait le sillage et ne daignait rien voir.*

—in turn itself perhaps an echo of the more famous silence of Ajax in the *Odyssey*. What is common to all these cases is the interest of the poet and his readers in the human attitude, the sense of dramatic behaviour which human beings display in moments of crisis, disaster, or impending fear. And these attitudes are always instinctive and individual, not schooled by any intellectual process or by theories of what should be done.

Auden's variation upon this theme is to make this gesture frankly adolescent (some critics might argue that the tradition is in any case an adolescent one), and to centre the imagery and emotion of his poem in childhood experience. So far from being a call to arms, an assertion that we must get away from all this and acquire a new national identity and a new morale, the poem—as a *poem*—revels unashamedly in what we are and what we have.

> There's great delight in what we have.
> The rattle of pebbles on the shore
> Under the retreating wave.

Yeats is again an illuminating parallel. A child sees the images of disaster sharply and vividly, but irresponsibly; he does not seek to order or to understand the mess but simply adopts it as a private world, a world which gives satisfaction to his appetite and curiosity. A child might understand the silence of Ajax in hell, or rather respond in some intuitive way to its meaning, but he would not understand the causes of the Depression, the need for the elimination of the demoralised rentier class and for a change of heart that would produce a new idealism and a new dynamism in industrial relations, etc. The apparent *raison d'être* of the poem is thus in complete opposition to its effective world, 'the view from Birmingham to Wolverhampton', the private world of

⌈detailed nostalgia⌉ which haunts all Auden's earlier
poetry.

These points become clearer if we compare Auden's evocations of dead nightmare landscapes and approaching doom
with those of T. S. Eliot in *The Rock* and in *Burnt Norton*.

> *Men and bits of paper, whirled by the cold wind*
> *That blows before and after time,*
> *Wind in and out of unwholesome lungs*
> *Time before and time after.*
> *Eructation of unhealthy souls*
> *Into the faded air, the torpid*
> *Driven on the wind that sweeps the gloomy hills of London,*
> *Hampstead and Clerkenwell, Campden and Putney,*
> *Highgate, Primrose, and Ludgate. Not here*
> *Not here in the darkness, in this twittering world.*
>
> (*Burnt Norton*)

Here the nightmare is a real one, and the images, related if
not to a central philosophy at least to a central *tone* of
thought, are subordinate and obedient—they do not fight
against the overt intention of the poem in the obstreperous
delight of being themselves. The note is grave, prophetic,
full of distaste; and the absence of vitality is accompanied by
a curious absence of originality—the Old Testament and
Blake's prophetic books, particularly the first section of Jeru-
salem, are visible adjuncts to the traditional mode of writing
which Eliot employs. By contrast, and in spite of the metrical debt to Tennyson, Auden's poem makes a brilliantly and
strikingly individual impact. But it has the vision of a child,
at once neutral and passionate, while Eliot's poem has the
controlled, fatigued, but 'engaged' outlook of the middle-
aged man. Nor is the difference simply one of the poet's age
at the time the poem is written.

The dispossessed imagination may suffer from the lack of an intellectual tradition to set in order the experiences which impinge upon it. The adolescent imagination does not so suffer, because it is not called upon to judge what it experiences by any other standard than its own intensity. Hence the success, in a Romantic period, of the youthful talent, like that of Shelley or Keats: at a later date the boy prodigy becomes even more exaggeratedly youthful—a Rimbaud or a Raymond Radiguet. These were talents who succeeded because they grew up quickly, but their success prompted the question: why grow up at all? The cult of childhood in writing, its emotions and its private symbols, is one that is still with us today in consequence. The child was of course an important figure in early Romantic theory, as Wordsworth's *Immortality Ode* shows, but his position was a symbolic one: he was not valued for himself, but by a sort of inverted Platonist process he came to seem the possessor of truths which for the adult had faded into the light of common day. Moreover his position and function were quite overt and official—Shelley can compare himself to a tired child without giving the game away. But in Auden's poetry, as in much modern literature, the adolescent note—however strong and shaping its influence—is never admitted to be such. The closest that Auden has come to such an admission is his fondness for a Nietzsche quotation— 'Maturity—to recover the seriousness one had as a child at play'—and his references to poetry as a particular sort of game.

Yeats's creation of 'Crazy Jane' gives us a clue to the importance of the adolescent outlook in modern poetry and in Auden's in particular. For Yeats, the fool figure, who in madness and simplicity has instinctive wisdom, has much deliberate meaning and is deliberately created; but two implications are of particular interest to us: Crazy Jane defies authority, and she is fully 'human' where her betters are not. Both these characteristics emerge strongly in the early poem of Auden from which we have quoted, though in an indirect way. 'Authority' is at once the industrial concerns, the wreckage of which so much fascinates the poet, and the august 'boon companions' who have betrayed us and at whom we can now cock a snook (the list of them is quite indiscriminate, as well as being chattily private, and includes at least two names who either were, or were to become, heroes of Auden). [The human attitude resides in the poem's effective pleasure in the monstrous corpse of industry; in the accusation at one's betters that they don't really know what Life is; and in the complex gesture of nostalgia and self-acceptance which is made in the childhood image of watching the rain fall on the sea.] An apparently denunciatory poem about industry and politics in fact makes its impact in very much the same way as one of Yeats's Crazy Jane poems, and it makes it by a use—how conscious a use one cannot say— of the attitudes and images of adolescence; for in an age of ideology and mechanisation only the child remains unmechanised and human.

Naturally the word 'human' is a question-begging one. Why, it may be objected, should one possible activity, like *Schadenfreude* or making a graceful or derisive gesture, be more 'human' than another, like setting one's ideas in order, social planning, and worrying about the future? 'Spontaneous' or what Yeats understood by 'passionate' would perhaps be better words. Keats, speaking of the 'instinctive attitudes' of the human creature as poetry's subject, was probably thinking of the same thing. If the word is given this sense, however, it is incredible that Yeats and Auden should frequently have been criticised for being 'inhuman' in their poetry. In the case of Auden especially, such an accusation seems to imply a complete failure to appreciate his poetry and to see what it essentially is.

But there are reasons for this misunderstanding. For the whole tenor of Auden's critical pronouncements on poetry has been to imply a separation between the poet as Poet, and as a responsible social being commanded to love his neighbour and behave properly, and do what he can to establish what Auden calls The Just City. The poet can indulge in all the romantic attitudes: the man must conform to the classical moral pattern. Although this dualism would have been quite intelligible to Bacon and Plato, it has never been so abruptly stated by a poet. Auden makes the distinction again and again, until we are left wondering if his obsession with it indicates some uneasiness of conscience. Why should he stress so continually that Art is one thing and Life is another, and that nothing but bad art and wrong living will come if we try to mix the two? The romantic theory of their separation is of course already well known to us: for Poe and Housman it was a necessary and comfortable one, of advantage to both sides. Housman's citing of the unpoetic phrase from the New Testament which is none the less 'the greatest discovery of the moral world', and his contention that when we say we admire poetry we are often admiring something *in* it—these are confident assertions of the romantic attitude. Auden's is more deeply considered and less confident, but in a sense no less uncompromising. He sees Art as a mirror world, complete in every detail, the only difference between it and the real world being that it does not in fact exist. In Art, as Caliban puts it in *The Sea and the Mirror*, 'all the phenomena of an empirically ordinary world are given. Extended objects appear to which events happen—old men catch dreadful coughs, little girls get their arms twisted. . . .

All the voluntary movements are possible—crawling through flues and old sewers, sauntering past shopfronts, tiptoeing through quicksands and mined areas, running through derelict factories and across empty plains . . . all the modes of transport are available, but any sense of direction, any knowledge of where on earth one has come from or where on earth one is going to, is completely absent.'

Art is thus a frozen world, locked in a series of gestures which, though fascinating and arresting, remain necessarily disconnected with the continuity of living. Of course there is a clear sense in which this is true—what happens in a book, or on the stage or screen, may be 'exactly like life', but it cannot become it. But, we feel like asking, so what? Is this premise so very important? Does it lead us anywhere? Why should it need so much reiteration? The great classical writers would not have even considered it worth saying; Dante, Goethe, and Tolstoy are not disturbed by the aware-ness that what they write is not Life: they are preoccupied rather with the points at which Art and Life touch and interact, with the interplay of influence and resemblance, not with the initial, if basic, dissimilarity.

Why should this dissimilarity haunt Auden so much? Per-haps because he cannot really persuade himself that the way in which he likes to write, and the subject, the *ambiance* which liberate him into writing, have much to do with the part of himself that actually lives from day to day, that has come from somewhere and is going to somewhere else. Dickens, say, never appears to have been struck by such a realisa-tion: as a novelist he seems to have complete confidence that his day-dream world and its inhabitants are as real—perhaps more real—than the stream of facts, decisions and problems that confronted him in the daily process of living. And Sartre, to take a very different example, seems to have com-

plete confidence in the relevance to actual life of his imaginary hero Antoine Roquentin. But Auden seems to have no
such confidence in his creations. The situations that appear
and recur in his poems with such vividness are of the kind
which we can imagine occurring to the poet as he closes his
eyes for a liberating instant between two minutes of actual
living. They are glimpses of life, brilliantly concrete, but
seen from the unparticipating outside, as we see the screen
when sitting in the cinema. They are 'the *voluntary* movements'—'sauntering past shopfronts, tiptoeing through
quicksands and mined areas, running through derelict factories'.

> ... *Or smoking wait till hour of food*
> *Leaning on chained-up gate*
> *At edge of wood.*

> *Cigarette end smouldering on a border*
> *At the first garden party of the year.* ...

> *In strangled orchards and the silent comb*
> *Where dogs have worried or a bird was shot.*

> ... *the crooked claws*
> *Emerging into view and groping*
> *For handholds on the low round coping,*
> *As horror clambers from the well.*

> *The smiling grimy boy at the garage*
> *Ran out before he blew his horn.* ...

> *Where country curates in cold bedrooms*
> *Dreamed of deaneries till at daybreak*
> *The rector's rooks with relish described*
> *Their stinted station.*

Altogether elsewhere, vast
Herds of reindeer move across
Miles and miles of golden moss,
Silently and very fast.

The cat has died at Ivy Dene,
The Crowthers' pimply son has passed Matric,
St Neots has put up light blue curtains,
Frankie is walking out with Winnie
And Georgie loves himself.

Black currant bushes hide the ruined opera house where badgers are said to breed in great numbers; an old horse-tramway winds away westward through suave foothills crowned with stone circles . . . to the north, beyond a forest inhabited by charcoal burners one can see the Devil's Bedposts quite distinctly; to the east, the museum where for sixpence one can touch the ivory chessmen.

All these extracts have in common the fact of seeming to take place 'altogether elsewhere'; though they are introduced for different reasons and in different tones—ironic, lyrical, allegoric—they all exist startlingly clear of their contexts. Their resemblance to film technique, and in particular to the film close-up, is obvious (the cigarette-end smouldering in the border, the 'frozen buzzard flipped over weir')— Auden has worked in films and shares with Christopher Isherwood an interest in their technique of style and build-up. Isherwood tells in *Lions and Shadows* an autobiographical story into which Auden enters, how he would go again and again to bad films simply to observe how characters walked across a room, lit a cigarette or waited at a bus-stop. This interest in the stylisation of 'humanness' is not of course unrelated to the poem's theme, just as it is not unrelated in the film, even though one may suspect that in both it takes its origin from the child's unreflective and wholehearted anthropomorphism of everything that comes into its orbit. The objects in the child's world are associated either with safety and calm or with terror and fascination—a fearful joy: and the two lie side by side. Tennyson's 'dreadful hollow behind the little wood' is as necessary to the child's intense perception of its environment as Auden's 'patriarchs wiser than Abraham who mended their nets on the modest wharf'. As necessary, and yet as disconnected with any rational sense of the place in a total scheme of things of dreadful hollows and fishermen patriarchs. As the quotation shows (and Auden has commented on Tennyson's infantile approach to poetry with the knowingness of the man who recognises his obsession commenting on the man who doesn't), Tennyson felt the effectiveness of 'fearful joy' in securing the poetic assent of the reader. Auden recognises it much more consciously; makes use of it, makes fun of it, analyses it, distrusts it. We are separated from childhood, he hints, as we are separated from art. We can never get back there and it is disastrous to try. The moods appropriate to childhood and to poetry cannot be permitted free play in a grown-up world and a responsible society. 'All poets', he says in an essay, 'adore explosions, thunderstorms, tornadoes, conflagrations, ruins, scenes of spectacular carnage. The poetical imagination is therefore not at all a desirable quality in a chief of state.' All poets with the particular romantic bent of Auden, one might qualify, and such a poet also adores private languages, schoolboy symbols, sinister landscapes in which hikers and waiters are really spies and agents of the Adversary or 'They', and 'amusing ourselves on what would otherwise have been a very dull evening indeed by planning to seize the post office across the river'.

And so, as he says in another essay, ['there must always be two kinds of art—escape art, for man needs escape as he needs food and deep sleep, and parable art, that art which shall teach man to unlearn hatred and learn love'] The dichotomy so stated seems one of almost staggering crudity. Is there indeed no middle way between the 'altogether elsewhere' where 'the minotaur of authority is just a roly-poly ruminant and nothing is at stake', and art which is consciously connected with some ethical scheme for our betterment? Not for the poet, would seem to be Auden's reply, and indeed in his own poetic development and practice the dichotomy is very marked: his critical bluntness seems to arise from the *fait accompli* of his own work and its individual quality. Perhaps for the novelist though: Auden has always venerated this form of art, in which the phenomenology of life can be seen steadily and commented on *in extenso*. 'A higher art than poetry altogether', he calls it in one of his *Letters to Lord Byron*, and in his sonnet *The Novelist* he says that the poet, 'encased in talent like a uniform', can dash forward like a hussar or amaze us like a thunderstorm, but cannot, he implies, do very much else. The suggestion of talent—perhaps the gift of conveying the delight of a private world or a private game—as an *insulator*, is as revealing as the thunderstorm image: Auden has already told us that the poet adores such displays. But it is different for the novelist.

> *For, to achieve his lightest wish, he must*
> *Become the whole of boredom, subject to*
> *Vulgar complaints like love, among the Just*
>
> *Be just, among the Filthy filthy too,*
> *And in his own weak person, if he can,*
> *Must suffer dully all the wrongs of Man.*

This deprecation of poetry—'the old innocent game of play-

ing God with words'—is not a defensive or obscurantist attitude in Auden: he does not imply, as Romantics like Housman did—that poetry is a pure mystery to be kept separate
from the vulgar hurly-burly of affairs. Nor is it like music,
of which Auden observes

> *Only your notes are pure contraption,*
> *Only your song is an absolute gift.*

Music, like Housman's poetry, may 'cascade'—in Auden's
enchanting phrase—'the falls of the knee and the weirs of the
spine', but poetry is rather different, not pure contraption
but robust game. None the less,

> The gulf between frivolity and seriousness, between
> choosing to obey the rules of a game which it does not
> matter whether you play or not, and choosing to obey the
> rules of life which you have to live whether you like it or
> not, and where the rules are necessary because they do not
> cease to exist if you disobey them but operate within you
> to your own destruction—this gulf is so infinite that all
> talk about children's games being a preparation for adult
> life is misleading twaddle.
>
> *(Squares and Oblongs)*

The game is not a preparation for adult life; the attitudes of
poetry are not valid in living. Again we feel inclined to retort: 'But you are thinking of your own poetry, or of poetry
that in some way resembles it.' Is Auden taking this Platonic
line because Romantic poetry, *if taken seriously* and allowed
to influence our attitudes to life, may encourage vicious attitudes, and put itself, as T. S. Eliot might say, at the service
of unacceptable ideas? Certainly it is possible to imagine the
poetry of Shelley, say (which Auden detests), or that of
Housman or Yeats, exercising a temporary influence over

the behaviour of the young which could be called a bad influence. Suicides may have followed from a perusal of the *Shropshire Lad*. In Japan, where translations of Housman are popular, they no doubt have. Yeats's aesthetic attitude might be said to regard life as a game—'a test of inborn *aretē*' as Auden says about the Greek attitude to life—and such an *aretē* of stylish toughness rather than stylish sensitivity might appeal to would-be aesthetes who had begun to find Pater rather old-fashioned. But this point is clearly a minor one: as soon as one considers specific instances, the question of whether poetry is or is not capable of 'doing harm' becomes quite unreal. Whether or not one finds significance in Auden's view of poetry as a voluntary game and life as an involuntary task, one finds no difficulty in agreeing that poetry is not ideology. It is far too complete, the formal, pattern, or 'game' aspect of it is much too important, for its 'ideas' to have free play. Auden despises Shelley for having called poets 'the unacknowledged legislators of the world' and says that such a description fits the secret police better. Or, one might add, the great ideologues. The ideas of Rousseau, Nietzsche, and Marx have had a much more obvious and drastic effect on human behaviour than the poetry of either Shelley or Shakespeare.

None the less, Auden is surely wrong in maintaining that because of the 'gratuitous' nature of poetry it has nothing to teach us about life and can only do harm if it tries. The potential harm consists in treating the writing—and presumably the reading—of poetry 'as if it were a kind of religious technique, a way of learning to be happy and good'. The distinction is surely too simple. If poetry is not religion must it therefore be a game? Even if it is, why the existential sternness of this complete divorce between games and life?— the latter is for most people a sufficiently complex affair to

142

include the former. Manners, customs, all the sane ceremonial of living, could easily be called a game according to
Auden's definition: yet they occupy an important place in
life, and poetry as a part of them surely deserves to be considered, to use an old-fashioned phrase, as a civilising
influence?

In another context, and with the inconsistency which is
such an endearing feature of Yeats's critical attitudes, Auden
virtually admits this. He writes in the notes to the *New Year
Letter*:

> Wagner is perhaps the greatest genius that ever lived.
> But in the expression of suffering only. Happiness, social
> life, mystical joy, success, were completely beyond him.
> For spontaneous happiness, friendship, requited love, we
> must go elsewhere—to Mozart.
>
> For the strong, the intelligent, the healthy, the success-
> ful, those on whom, just because they are so, falls the duty
> of understanding weakness, stupidity, disease and failure
> in order that they may cure them, Wagner's operas are
> essential, a constant source of delight. They *must* listen
> to him.
>
> But who should never be allowed to listen to Wagner?
> The unhappy, the disappointed, the politically ambitious,
> the self-pitying, those who imagine themselves misunder-
> stood, the Wagnerians. And to whom should they be
> compelled to listen?—to Mozart and Beethoven.

What has happened to music as pure contraption, as absolute
gift? And Mozart emerges as the musician of social graces
and games, of civilised and happy living, who is therapeutic
in effect for precisely this reason. Art takes on the nature not
of a game but of occupational therapy. We can imagine the
neurotic being submitted to a course not of Mozart only,

but of Ariosto, Gay, Calverley, and the *Oxford Book of Light Verse*. The civilising influence becomes a compulsory routine, while Auden seems to regard with equanimity the idea that we might be conditioned to benefit from art which makes no instinctive appeal to our temperament.

Although they may at times be inconsistent, all Auden's ideas about art and poetry are extremely forthright; there are no hesitations or qualifications, and as we have seen from the contrast he draws between 'escape art' and 'parable art' he is never afraid of being graphic, even crude. The violence of his contrasts comes from his dependence on two sources of theory: first, Freud, and second, Kierkegaard and the Existentialists—the influence of the second increasing as that of the first has waned. Freud saw art as a substitute for power where the artist was concerned, a substitute in fantasy for what the artist's disposition denied him in life—'power, honour, riches, and the love of women'. And though there is for the artist 'a path back to reality' it lies in revealing for his public 'the comfort and consolation of their own unconscious sources of pleasure', and hence winning in fact by his reputation the rewards that life had previously denied him. Art, moreover, 'seldom dares to make any attack on the realm of reality'. Auden in his earlier work accepts and makes frequent references to Freud's point of view. Michael Ransom in *The Ascent of F6* censures Dante in typically Freudian terms.

It was not Virtue those lips, which involuntary privation had made so bitter, could pray for; it was not Knowledge; it was Power. Power to exact for every snub, every headache, every unfallen beauty, an absolute revenge; wit with a stroke of the pen to make a neighbour's vineyard a lake of fire and to create in his private desert the austere music of the angels or the happy extravagance of a fair.

In a later essay Auden has added a significant gloss to this:

> In primitive societies the incantation of a curse is be-
> lieved to be practically as effective as a stab with a knife,
> but aesthetics only begins when it is realised that one man
> curses another because he knows that he is unable to
> murder him.
>
> (*Mimesis and Allegory*.)

'*Because* he knows'—Auden's conviction of the sharply self-
conscious processes in the author's mind is certainly applic-
able to himself. No poet perhaps has ever been more determined to be conscious of what he is doing and his reasons
for doing it. And with Auden there is no gap between the
creator and the commentator, although there is frequently a
marked differentiation in *effect* between the joyous pursuit of
a phrase or image for its own sake and the part that it is intended to play in the reasoned dimension of the poem. When
he writes, for example, of the 'collarless herds who eat blanc-
mange and have never said anything witty', the charm of the
phrase is in the sheer unfairness and irresponsibility of its
gusto and wit. He is speaking of the Others, the dim
creatures, the masses outside the exclusive sparkle of the
gang. He cannot harm them by speaking of them in this way
—his own theory protects him there—and, conversely, a
kind of malice which must never be allowed in life is finding
in art a graceful and easy outlet. That is why, as Auden
reiterates again and again,

> . . . *these halcyon structures are useful*
> *As structures go—though not to be confused*
> *With anything really important*
> *Like feeding strays or looking pleased when caught*
> *By a bore or a hideola.*
>
> (*Music is International*.)

'Be nice in life and in poetry you can be as nasty as you please'—the advice seems too clear-cut, too sanitative, too chilling, a kind of poetic *Ketman* which forbids life and literature to meet and mingle in the passionate and unselfconscious manner they once did.

And it has its practical disadvantages for the artist. It means we find it almost impossible to take him seriously. We can laugh at or with him; admire his technical brilliance and the virtuosity of his language; shudder delightfully at the images in which he embodies his private nightmares and connect them with those Freudian 'unconscious sources' of our own. But is this enough? Not only is Auden always intensely conscious of what he is doing: he makes us, his readers, equally conscious of what is happening to us, and how, and why. His clinical attitude prohibits the nebulous, the profundity which moves us but which we cannot quite grasp. Perhaps because, as he says,

> *What we find rousing or touching*
> *Tells us little and confuses us much. . . .*

and confusion is a dangerous frame of mind, leading to abuses and difficulties in the sphere of life. Auden does not seem to admit the existence of a Keatsian 'negative capability' in poetry, a state of fruitful uncertainty, of being on the edge of some truth whose centre we cannot from its very nature express. Only in one or two of his earliest poems—Numbers 18 and 19 in *Poems* 1930 for instance —does he seem to be poetically 'in the dark' and groping towards something which he cannot apprehend with precision.

He shares with T. S. Eliot this enormous self-consciousness—it is one of the few points which they have in common. In Eliot it takes the form of a deprecation, an honest enquiry, an implied refusal to posture before the reader and dazzle him with a display of poetical virtuosity.

> *That was a way of putting it—not very satisfactory,*
> *A periphrastic study in a worn-out poetical fashion*
> *Leaving one still with the intolerable wrestle*
> *With words and meanings. The poetry does not matter.*
>
> <div align="right">(<i>East Coker.</i>)</div>

Following a passage that is, as it were, wearily rhetorical and artificial ('What is the late November doing'), this disclaimer may baffle and irritate the reader, but it certainly leaves him in no doubt about the poet's honesty. It is almost a device for creating an atmosphere of sincerity. In Auden's case the fact that 'the poetry does not matter' is rather differently conveyed: the poet does not attempt to disguise the fact that he is a virtuoso whose job it is to give a good performance, but his gestures as he does so are ironical, and the irony is often directed at the poet himself. In both cases the idea that the poetry is important is not entertained, but whereas for Eliot the poetry is part of a general ethos which is of the very first importance, for Auden it is not. This is perhaps why we can take Eliot seriously even when he is being his most exasperatingly deprecating and self-conscious, whereas the Auden irony and urbanity we follow gladly for their own sake and can only be persuaded of their final seriousness by external means, i.e. by the subject matter—refugees, war, etc.—which the poet puts before us. Auden has always shown a great interest in light verse and the ironic approach, and we must return for a fuller examination of his methods here, but our point for the moment is the connection between such an approach and the contemporary poetic self-consciousness. Deprecation in Eliot, irony in Auden, are symptoms of the same condition.

147

Because of his brisk desire to make distinctions between life and art, escape and parable, the localising effects of this self-consciousness are much more apparent in Auden than in Eliot. Consider an image of Auden's which has been quoted before. It occurs in the *New Year Letter*, where Auden is illustrating the theological concept that Man's life is a state of Becoming, not of Being, and that though accidental 'spots of time' may occur in which he can sample the perfection of Being he must not try to stay in this condition or prolong it, or else

> *The sky grows crimson with a curse*
> *The flowers change colour for the worse,*
> *He hears behind his back the wicket*
> *Padlock itself, from the dark thicket*
> *The chuckle with no healthy cause,*
> *And, helpless, see the crooked claws*
> *Emerging into view and groping*
> *For hand-holds on the low round coping,*
> *As Horror clambers from the well:*
> *For he has sprung the trap of Hell.*

> (*New Year Letter.*)

The image is delightful, but it is pure M. R. James. Its associations for the reader are of a quite different kind from those explanatory concepts of Being and Becoming which Auden with his usual virtuosity deploys. Whatever we feel when we try to prolong the moment 'at the still point of the turning world', as Eliot calls it, it would surely not be this: the world where such *frissons* of cheerful horror occur is all too obviously the normal day-to-day world. The images of possession and loss in which Eliot, on the other hand, describes a similar order of experience in the *Four Quartets* does seem to coincide at a deep level with what we may ourselves have felt about such experience.

> *Then a cloud passed, and the pool was empty.*
> > *(Burnt Norton.)*
>
> *Dawn points, and another day*
> *Prepares for heat and silence. Out at sea the dawn wind*
> *Wrinkles and slides.*
> > *(East Coker.)*

'No artist', writes Auden, 'not even Eliot, can prevent his work being used as magic, for that is what all of us, high-brow and lowbrow alike, secretly want Art to be'. And it is a guilty secret.

> *Shame at our shortcomings makes*
> *Lame magicians of us all,*
> *Forcing our invention to*
> *An illegal miracle*
> *And a theatre of disguise. . . .*
> > *(Epithalamion.)*

The shame of Magic is that it solves easily what in life can only be solved partially and with continual effort. And this consciousness of the possibility of poetry being used as an incantation, as a quick way to a satisfaction of the feelings, haunts Auden, perhaps because the 'magical' power of his own poetry is so obvious and so impressive. But it is a quick self-contained 'magical' satisfaction that the Auden quotation, divorced from its context, gives us, and though the poet is careful to dissipate such impressions as much as he can by descent into irony—'wit that spoils Romantic art', as he calls it—or into flat statement or exhortation, it is the 'magical' passages that remain with the reader. Irony does not necessarily destroy magic, for, as we shall see later, it may itself be one of magic's expedients. What does destroy it is Eliot's deliberate and weary refusal to keep up the incantation: by shrugging his shoulders with a 'that was a way of putting it' he effectively checks any attempt of the reader to repose in an insulated enjoyment of the passage. And at what a cost! If this is a preventive against magic, we should have good grounds for preferring magic instead. Whether true or not, Auden's admission that magic is what we want poetry to be gives the clue to the real source of vitality in his own poetry.

None the less, Auden's attitude implies a certain desperation. How can 'magic' and parable ever be reconciled by a poet who is so obsessed with the difference between them? How can our reaction be anything but ambiguous towards a poetry that is by implication telling us: 'I may read like a charm but you must not take me for one. My subject is Love, the Just City, right conduct, the nature of moral and religious choice, etc.' Dante's subject was not dissimilar— the nature of the universe, of the highest wisdom and divine love—but we cannot imagine Dante concerned about the way in which this might be mistaken for, or taken as, an autotelic charm, a surrogate power and glory. It might be argued that many, if not most, of Dante's readers today do in fact take it as such, and that Auden is only being realistic in admitting this, but there is all the difference between a poetry that is not composed in the expectation that the reader will rest upon its qualities in a kind of aesthetic full-stop, finding in them 'the consolation of his own unconscious sources of pleasure', and a poetry which secretly admits that this will probably happen.

Nor is the rigour of the dichotomy apparently lessened by existentialist theories of art. 'One must get out of the poetical into the existential' is one of Auden's favourite

Kierkegaard quotations; another, 'the poet's sin is to poeti-
cise instead of being'. And by implication it is his readers,
sin to read the poetry instead of living. In Kierkegaard the
Aesthetic and the Ethical are sharply divided—two stages
from one to the other of which the individual must move.
And Sartre is similarly emphatic. 'The real is never beautiful', he writes. 'Beauty is a value which can apply only to
the imaginary, and whose essential structure involves the
nullification of the world. This is why it is foolish to confuse ethics and aesthetics. The values of the Good presuppose
being-in-the-world; they are concerned with behaviour in
real contexts and are subject from the start to the essential
absurdity of existence.' The debt of Auden's critical outlook
to pronouncements of this type is obvious, and it is this bleak
critical climate which is accepted in the context of his poems.
And not only accepted, but exploited sometimes with a
positive buoyancy. Auden delights in turning into poetry—
in 'nullifying' into the poetic as Sartre might call it—the
most ragged and 'viscous' aspects and experiences of life. He
seems to find its randomness and existential absurdity a challenge to his skill. *The Age of Anxiety* is particularly full of
such passages.

> *In a vacant lot*
> *We built a bonfire and burned alive*
> *Some stolen tyres. How strong and good one*
> *Felt at first, how fagged coming home through*
> *The urban evening. Heavy like us*
> *Sank the gas-tanks—it was supper time.*
> *In hot houses helpless babies and*
> *Telephones gabbled untidy cries,*
> *And on embankments black with burnt grass*
> *Shambling freight-trains were shunted away*
> *Past crimson clouds.*

The brilliancy of description ends there. It does not lead anywhere—(indeed it is difficult to see where anything in *The
Age of Anxiety* can be said to lead)—but it conveys a sense of
the occasion at once and with vivid accuracy, and gives the
reader the unpursuing satisfaction of contemplating a formal
triumph. It is difficult for the most conscientious reader—if
he enjoys the passage at all—not to repose upon the event
described, upon its sense of the particular and upon the
flavour of nostalgic recollection which it holds. A comparison with Eliot is again legitimate and illuminating. *Preludes*
are equally careful evocations of the shabby and incomplete
urban moment.

> *The burnt-out ends of smoky days.*
> *And now a gusty shower wraps*
> *The grimy scraps*
> *Of withered leaves about your feet*
> *And newspapers from vacant lots;*
> *The showers beat*
> *On broken blinds and chimney-pots. . . .*

But the poet not only has a general and 'ethical' comment
to make on this world ('the notion of some infinitely gentle,
infinitely suffering thing')—he is also eager to put us in
touch with his own *feelings* about the thing described and
hence to induce a corresponding feeling, perhaps of depression or indignation, in us, which will lead us away from
aesthetic satisfaction and back to the emotions of daily life.
This is not the case in Auden. Magic persists, with the tacit
encouragement of the author, who 'cannot prevent' his work
being used in this way.

Expert in self-diagnosis, Auden has even indicated how
the 'unromantic' and satirical approach can itself lead to the
state of aesthetic equilibrium and completeness which con-

stitutes Magic. The more perceptive and unified the approach, the greater the chance that the intelligent reader will simply sit back and enjoy the situation, will enjoy particularly the dazzling *mots* and turns of phrase that mock at him for so enjoying it! As Caliban puts it in *The Sea and the Mirror*:

> In representing to you your condition of estrangement from the truth, (the poet) is doomed to fail the more he succeeds, for the more truthfully he paints the condition, the less clearly can he indicate the truth from which it is estranged, and, worse still, the more sharply he defines the estrangement itself—and, ultimately, what other aim and justification has he, what else exactly *is* the artistic gift which he is forbidden to hide, if not to make you unforgettably conscious of the ungarnished offended gap between what you so questionably are and what you are commanded without any question to become, of the unqualified No that opposes your every step in any direction?—the more he must strengthen your delusion that an awareness of the gap is itself a bridge, your interest in your imprisonment a release, so that, far from your being led by him to contrition and surrender, your dialogue, using his words, with yourself about yourself, becomes the one activity which never, like devouring or collecting or spending, lets you down, the one game which can be guaranteed, whatever the company, to catch on. . . .

With this penetrating piece of defeatism, Auden voices his own doubts about his poetry. Of what use is the most biting irony, the most urgent moral tone, if they are to be regarded as just two more delightful tricks in the craftsman's range? We agree, but we cannot help feeling that this very perspicacity shows the problem to be a little unreal—unreal, that is, to those who cannot see it so clearly because they are not accustomed to think of poetry as a subtle game of self-conscious nuances between poet and reader. If we take the T. S. Eliot quotation just referred to, are we conscious after reading it of the issue which Caliban puts with such Jamesian elaboration? If the poetry and the poet's feelings move us, then they move us, and not in so different a way from the manner in which the actual experiences described might have done. The poet's 'notion' is not so different from the one which we might have had: that, at any rate, is our feeling if we have enjoyed and admired the poem, and we should have a similar impression after reading a poem of Wordsworth or many others.

But with Auden we do not. Where his poetry is concerned Caliban's case has real cogency, for he does appear as the poet of a highly self-conscious private conspiracy between poet and reader, and no one is more conscious of this than Auden himself. But 'awareness of a gap is not a bridge', and the poet must endure this self-consciousness just as the reader, if he is fully to appreciate the poetry, must understand it. Critics of Auden have always appeared to find it difficult to talk about his poetry, as opposed to the borrowed materials in it, and its nominal pre-occupations: it is this that makes even a serious and informed critical approach seem so curiously beside the point. Thus Richard Hoggart often writes in his excellent study of the poet in a manner which would seriously mislead an uninformed but intelligent poetry reader—say a foreigner—about what the *actual* virtues of Auden's poetry are.

Auden combines an intense interest in the human heart with a desire to reform society, and he thinks our psychological ills greater than our political. . . . He is convinced of the urgent need for mental therapy; he believes that the spread and assimilation of the findings of psychology can help society towards health; he is sure that such action is morally desirable; he thinks it is owed to 'the human creature we must nurse to sense and decency'.

Accurate and unimpeachable statements. But how little relationship they bear to the reality of the verse! If, on the other hand, one were to write of T. S. Eliot's poetry like this, and for the same kind of reader, there would be no such gap. 'Eliot combines a strong interest in tradition and the Church and their possible place in modern society with a more personal preoccupation with the sources of peace and virtue for the individual in the understanding of time.' Such introductory remarks, though banal, would not be misleading, nor would the enquirer after reading them be startled by what he found in Eliot. One might sum up the matter by saying that while all Auden's apparently public, outgoing themes are in fact private and self-contained, Eliot's, even at their most exploratory and personal, retain a public susceptibility to exegesis and the straightforward explanatory gloss. To stress the inclusive and journalistic aspects of Auden's talent is in a sense as remote from his poetry as it would be to enumerate Mallarmé's subjects or Poe's attitudes to life and society.

I do not mean by this that Auden writes 'pure' poetry or anything approximating to it. But such poetry is undoubtedly a part of what he means by Magic, though in his case it is not the recherché affair of the Symbolists, but a distillation of his widespread interests and his fascination with place and people. Auden has followed Yeats in showing how the intense private world of symbolism can be brought right out into the open, eclecticised, and pegged down to every point of contemporary interest and everyday life, while remaining none the less in a private and even a substitute world. Auden is an emancipator of Romantic Symbolism, but it is in this tradition that his roots lie, and it is by the criteria applied to such poetry that he should ultimately be judged. Attacks on Auden are invariably based on his irresponsibility, his unfounded pretensions to intellectual power and weight, and his enjoyment of the private joke or absurdity for its own sake, etc., and all these strictures lose their force if his poetry is read for what it is, and not for what his critics—misled by the poet's ambiguous attitude—have supposed it is attempting to be.

Auden's is not public poetry in the sense in which Eliot's —even at its most meditative—can be said to be. But as we have seen, both poets share the extreme critical self-consciousness common among writers today, and it is for this reason that both can best be approached via their critical pronouncements and their attitude to poetry. We have examined some of the implications of Auden's criticism and applied it to his work in general. We must now make a more detailed survey of his poetic development as it is revealed in individual poems.

What makes a poem of Auden good or bad? The question, baldly put, can be as baldly answered: whether or not it is filled with vivid personal apprehensions of things—things and people, but above all things, for though Auden never regards people wantonly or inhumanly he does depersonalise them and transform them into a bizarre extension of object or place. Their significance to the poet as emblems of some general condition may be large, but they are always seen against some appropriate background or linked to their unique and revealing properties of clothing, accent, or facial tic. Auden is a Symbolist of the common fate, the humdrum situation. As soon as he generalises, steps out of the heightened world of the Symbolist's still life, his poetry sags and loses momentum. He speaks in the *New Year Letter* of '*Rilke whom Der Dinge bless, the Santa Claus of loneliness*', and just as Rilke was preoccupied in his poetry with *things* and their place in space, the space in which 'flowers endlessly prolong themselves', so Auden is absorbed in the spectacle of things and people in their medium of isolation. There are reasons for this medium—historical, social, or psychological—and these the poet sets himself to express with confidence and knowledge, but it is the vision itself that counts, and the fact that the poet has selected it, rather than that he can go on to give reasons for his selection.

It is a very English vision, as English as that of Dickens. Though clinical, it is also extremely parochial. And the ideal Auden reader should also have Dickensian tastes: he should be not unlike George Eliot's Mrs Linnet. Mrs Linnet was fond of reading the biographies of celebrated preachers, 'and wherever there was a predominance of Zion and the River of Life, she turned to the next page; but any passage in which she saw such promising nouns as "smallpox", "pony", or "boots and shoes", at once arrested her'. As a preacher, even though he rarely adopts in fact the 'loose immodest tone' of which he—with characteristic self-awareness—accuses himself, Auden can only expect to suffer the fate of Mrs Linnet's favourite divines. Any successful 'parable art' which he accomplishes is done through the medium of the boots and shoes, the pony and the smallpox, as it were, and this is very nearly equivalent to saying that Mallarmé's 'preaching' must be done through his swans and fauns and white pages, or Yeats's through Byzantium and the Gyres and the 'half-legendary' Irishmen of his imagination. Auden's mythology is as effective and magical as theirs, and as able to suggest dimensions of meaning in which the rationalising mind has little place.

Let us take what is perhaps the finest poem in Auden's first (1930) volume.

> Consider this, and in our time
> As the hawk sees it or the helmeted airman:
> The clouds rift suddenly—look there
> At cigarette-end smouldering on a border
> At the first garden party of the year.
> Pass on, admire the view of the massif
> Through plate glass windows of the Sport Hotel;
> Join there the insufficient units
> Dangerous, easy, in furs, in uniform
> And constellated at reserved tables
> Supplied with feelings by an efficient band
> Relayed elsewhere to farmers and their dogs
> Sitting in kitchens in the stormy fens.
>
> Long ago, supreme Antagonist,
> More powerful than the great northern whale
> Ancient and sorry at life's limiting defect,
> In Cornwall, Mendip, or the Pennine Moor
> Your comments on the highborn mining-captains
> Found they no answer, made them wish to die
> —Lie since in barrows out of harm.
> You talk to your admirers every day
> By silted harbours, derelict works,
> In strangled orchards, and the silent comb
> Where dogs have worried or a bird was shot.
> Order the ill that they attack at once:
> Visit the ports and interrupting
> The leisurely conversation in the bar
> Within a stone's throw of the sunlit water,

Beckon your chosen out. Summon
Those handsome and diseased youngsters, those women
Your solitary agents in the country parishes;
And mobilise the powerful forces latent
In soils that make the farmer brutal
In the infected sinus, and the eyes of stoats.
Then, ready, start your rumour, soft
But horrifying in its capacity to disgust
Which, spreading magnified, shall come to be
A polar peril, a prodigious alarm,
Scattering the people, as torn-up paper
Rags and utensils in a sudden gust,
Seized with immeasurable neurotic dread.

. . all who follow
The convolutions of your simple wish,
It is later than you think; nearer that day
Far other than that distant afternoon
Amid rustle of frocks and stamping feet
They gave the prizes to the ruined boys.
You cannot be away, then, no
Not though you pack to leave within an hour,
Escaping humming down arterial roads:
The date was yours; the prey to fugues,
Irregular breathing and alternate ascendancies
After some haunted migratory years
To disintegrate on an instant in the explosion of mania
Or lapse for ever into a classic fatigue.

The great virtue of this poem is its impassivity. The measured blank verse has unhurried power, quickening to a menacing tempo ('Then, ready, start your rumour . . .') or sinking easily into a bland sardonic commentary ('Relayed elsewhere to farmers and their dogs . . .'). Auden tells us in

Letters from Iceland that he has never 'understood' punctuation in poetry, and uses it simply as a breathing mark and to indicate how the speech of a poem should be broken up. This explains some of the syntactic difficulty in the poem—we should expect a comma after *whale*, and the long dash before *Lie since in barrows out of harm* is puzzling, but normal grammatical syntax is not necessarily required by the tone of grave declamation: Auden's early poetry is frequently based on spoken rather than written syntax, and he has the precedent both of Hopkins and of the French symbolists here. Moreover, as Isherwood tells us, his early poems were often based on a selection of the best lines in poems which were initially much longer.

The poem's calm and detached tone contrasts remarkably with the fever and dread it describes. As so often, Auden is describing present-day society as if it were seen by a schizophrenic, indeed as a schizophrenic would see any society and any of life's phenomena. Everything is transformed by this vision, which is not so different from the vision of a skilful camera in a film whose subject is the sinister, and which achieves the effect of mounting tension by such devices as the close-up of the cigarette-end and the shots of a crowd spilling out into the street. *The helmeted airman* is a typical compression of ancient and modern suggestion: there is a similar use in *Spain*—

Yesterday the assessment of insurance by cards . . . the invention
Of cartwheels and clocks, the taming of horses . . .

and the *highborn mining-captains* strengthen the idea of some mysterious military aristocracy which is one of Auden's early fascinations. He is fond, too, of placing the natural and the man-made worlds together. *The hawk or the helmeted airman* is echoed by a line from the poem in memory of Yeats:

The brooks were frozen, the airports almost deserted.

As the camera's eye roves, the commentator shifts from the suave and expository to the urgent, and back again. The *supreme Antagonist* is our old friend the Death Wish, the individual's unconscious desire for extinction which hastens the decay of a society which has become conscious of it. The Death Wish is a force frequently met with in Auden's early poems and in many vivid guises, a force whose coming— like that of the Furies or certain kinds of nightmare—is at once dreaded and desired. This ambivalence of feeling is particularly effective when Auden identifies himself with both sides, with the doomed order and with the forces of progress, as in the poem later called *Which Side am I supposed to be on?* He wants both to run with the hare and hunt with the hounds, and the desire for a triumph and a defeat equally vicarious and in which

> . . . *the live quarry all the same*
> *Were changed to huntsmen in the game*

is very close to the Freudian view of art. As for Freud, Love or Eros is Auden's positive force, Death the negative, and both are necessary human urges. Auden socialises them, so to speak, in his early poems, identifying the Eros drive with the approaching victory of communism and the new order, the Death Wish with the corrupt and pathetic world of financiers, heart-strangling suburbs, and prize-givings where the boys are already 'ruined'. Eros will solve not only social but personal problems (here Auden's debt to D. H. Lawrence and Homer Lane comes in)—and the poet's imagination sees the two as virtually synonymous—neuroses, misfits, and loneliness are products of a bourgeois era.

As a theory this will perhaps not bear very close examination, and the graphic imagery in which Auden conveys it should also not be looked into too closely. We have noticed already the lack of correspondence between idea and image in Auden, the escaping of the latter from the former's control, as in the quotation from *New Year Letter* on page 148. Similarly, though the picture of society at the mercy of a Death Wish which shows itself in numerous small symptoms and exercises a hypnotic fascination (the stoat simile is a good detail here) is brilliantly done, we may wonder whether such an antagonist is best symbolised by a kind of secret service chief, with all the associations of conscious *intelligence* and awareness, surely unsuited to such a dark unconscious force? And why should the allies of the Wish be solitary women in country parishes? For no sociological reason, surely, but because such women are obvious targets in a private game of curiosity and make-believe. And though it is appropriate that the moribund should be 'supplied with feelings' the only reason for their being 'insufficient' seems to be the contrast the word affords with the 'efficient band' three lines later. The word 'utensils', too, seems chosen because it is suitably grotesque rather than because it describes anything visually apprehended. A phrase in another poem— *First spring flowers arriving smashed*—achieves its effect of symbolised violence at the same cost of abstracting visual and sensuous accuracy. All Auden's imagery, even at its most startling and original, shows this tendency towards abstraction: it is as if the depersonalising process, permitting the reader to enjoy the image without making any emotional connection from it, were one of the 'rules of the game'. And as we shall see, this process becomes more marked as Auden's poetry develops.

On the other hand, some phrases in the poem reveal, as we examine them, a genuine metaphysical richness. *The*

convolutions of your simple wish is one; Auden can achieve
great depth and precision of meaning by the use of contrast-
ing nouns and adjectives. *Human on my faithless arm—the low
thud of the defunct*—lovers who *warm each other with their
wicked hands*—such phrases abound, and often carry a second
charge of meaning behind their obvious glitter. But we must
beware of taking this kind of meaningfulness as a criterion
of excellence, as we might in a real metaphysical writer. To
do so would be to judge Auden far too narrowly, dismissing
a high percentage of his effects as slick and superficial. In
fact, as with Dylan Thomas, the range of his poetic effects is
almost bewilderingly varied: we must not expect either poet
to be always one thing or the other, cerebral or incantatory,
romantic or intellectual—and we must read Auden in the
way we read Swinburne as well as in the way we read Donne
or Cleveland: his eclecticism is one of his most outstanding
features. The 'leisurely conversation in the bar Within a
stone's throw of the sunlit water' is a good example. We can
go to work on the phrase if we choose and lift its suggestiveness on to the rational level. Water is always an emblem of
liberation, happiness, 'straightening-out', in Auden's poetry,
and the juxtaposition of *stone* is significant—'Stop behaving
like a stone'. The implication is that the Good Place, the
right attitude, are not far away if we want to find them. But
is this line of analysis really very profitable? It only draws
attention to what might be a weakness in the poem—Auden
accepts the Freudian Death Wish, an inevitable and universal
part of the Psyche, and yet identifies it with a sickness of
society which can and must be cured—'If we really want to
live we'd better start at once to try.' Logically speaking, the
central image contradicts itself at its source. But this does
not affect the strength of the poem, for Auden's image is not
a metaphysical one, like Donne's famous compasses, estab-

lishing a logically coherent analogy, but a romantic one, employing its symbolic illustration in the manner indicated by Auden himself in *The Enchaféd Flood*.

A symbol is felt to be such before any possible meaning is consciously recognised, i.e., an object or event which is felt to be more important than the reason can consciously explain is symbolic. Secondly, a symbolic correspondence is never one to one but always multiple, and different persons perceive different meanings.

This is in essentials a restatement of conventional symbolist doctrine, the suggestion of a meaning that cannot from its nature be explicitly stated. In this sense the phrase about 'the sunlit water' is successful, and the analytic approach, which can be confidently explicit about the precision of such a line as 'the convolutions of your simple wish', can add little to its suggestive invitation. Auden is equally at home with the modes of suggestion and delineation, and this virtuosity is rewarding to the reader who does not look exclusively for either one or the other method.

A good example of this power of combination is the Sonnet, No. 29 in *Look Stranger!*, later called *Meiosis*. At first it seems to present us with complexities which demand further readings. Love, that detached and rather theoretical Audenian force, has made a capture.

> —*though he fought for breath*
> *He struggled only to possess Another,*
> *The snare forgotten in the little death;*
> *Till You, the seed, to which he was a mother,*
> *That never heard of Love, through Love was free,*
> *While he within his arms a world was holding,*

To take the all-night journey under sea,
Work west and northward, set up building.

Cities and years constricted to your scope,
All sorrow simplified though almost all
Shall be as subtle when you are as tall:
Yet clearly in that 'almost' all his hope
That hopeful falsehood cannot stem with love
The flood on which all move and wish to move.

Meiosis, or *Litotes*, is the rhetorical figure which represents a
thing as being less than it is, and with this hint the meaning
of the octet can be arrived at without much difficulty. As
with all rhetorical conceits, the *significacio* may be involved
but it is quite explicit. *He*, the Lover, thinks only of possession, but in attaining its object he releases love, represented
in little by the seed, which is set free to perform its work,
constricting 'cities and years' to its scope. With the second
line of the sestet, however, the sonnet becomes all but impenetrable to rational analysis. Is *all sorrow* the direct object
of *cities and years*? When we recall Auden's punctuation
technique the comma seems to make this doubtful, but at
least it appears that 'Sorrow' is simplified by its meiosis as the
seed, though 'almost all' of it will, as it were, proliferate
again into complication as the seed expands into 'cities and
years'. And the figure of the lover now returns, apparently
hoping—on the ground that only 'almost all' sorrow will
re-emerge—that falsehood is incompatible with love.

This exegesis makes the sestet seem laborious and mysti-
fying, but when we read the sonnet at a normal speed we
are not conscious of being unduly baffled; the obscurity does
not check and irritate or demand to be sorted out; and we
float over it on to the final line with a satisfying impression
of the sonnet as a whole. It may not be a very clear im-

pression, but that is part of the poem's technique: indeed it is difficult not to conclude that Auden's purpose in the sestet is to give us the *feeling* of a complex idea rather than presenting such an idea for our rational elucidation; to give us a sort of metaphysical thrill which is implemented by the finicky precision of that *'almost'*, and clinched at each end by the octet's vigorous ending (echoing a line of Donne) and the broad Dantesque majesty of the concluding line. Love, we note, finds its way into the last line of Auden's poems with the same frequency that God does in Browning's.

As so often in Auden, film technique offers an analogy—in this case the kind of technical language that is used in a film for its realistic effect but without the audience needing to understand in detail what is being said. The use of an apparently metaphysical exactness of language for its suggestiveness, not for its literal meaning, is an invention of Auden's own, and he shows by it that the rational structure of wit poetry can be successfully combined with the suggestion of Symbolism. In his early poems Auden had not mastered this synthesis, and an air of bafflement is often the result—the poet seems baffled by the task of transmitting the experience no less than is the reader by the task of apprehending it. It was at this early stage that Auden used to assert that ' "understanding" a poem was not a logical process but a receiving, as a unity, a pattern of co-ordinated images that had sprung from free association of subconscious ideas, private to [the poet] himself'. But though the early poems to which this frankly symbolist process applies often have a kind of muffled vigour, Auden seems to have soon decided that the symbolist independence of syntax is a mistake, and that when 'the poet fetches the images out that hurt and connect', their connection must be grammatically coherent, that the reader must be reassured by the rational aspect of the poem until the 'receiving' process has worked on him. *Meiosis* is a good sonnet because it succeeds in being at once difficult and coherent, rational and suggestive. The way in which this balance is achieved may not commend itself to the critical analyst, but such a critic usually takes too narrow and rigorous a view, which he feels that Auden—in a supposedly 'intellectual' poem—should endorse.

None the less, there is a danger that Auden's mastery of equilibrium, of aesthetic balance, may become too artificial, a part of the tendency to depersonalise, to make every situation heraldic and self-contained, which we have already noticed. There is something direct and raw about a few of the early poems which the later skills which we have been examining quite eclipse.

> *It was Easter as I walked in the public gardens*
> *Hearing the frogs exhaling from the pond,*
> *Watching traffic of magnificent cloud*
> *Moving without anxiety on open sky—*
> *Season when lovers and writers find*
> *An altering speech for altering things,*
> *An emphasis on new names, on the arm*
> *A fresh hand with fresh power.*
> *But thinking so I came at once*
> *Where solitary man sat weeping on a bench,*
> *Hanging his head down, with his mouth distorted*
> *Helpless and ugly as an embryo chicken.*
>
> (*Poems* 1930. No. 16.)

The last lines, with their deliberate baldness, as ugly and clumsy as the scene they describe, disturb the reader. There is no suggestion here of the mirror world of art, with its magical capacity to turn all it sees to favour and to prettiness. We do not think of the separation between art and life

any more than we do in T. S. Eliot's *Preludes*, already referred to. But is not the baldness here rather too deliberate,
rather too calculatedly uncomfortable? An extract from
Dylan Thomas's poem *The Hunchback in the Park*, with its
odd coincidence of subject, will perhaps show what I am
getting at.

> *The hunchback in the park*
> *A solitary mister*
> *Propped between trees and water*
> *From the opening of the garden lock*
> *That lets the trees and water enter*
> *Until the Sunday sombre bell at dark*
>
> *Eating bread from a newspaper*
> *Drinking water from the chained cup*
> *That the children filled with gravel*
> *In the fountain basin where I sailed my ship*
> *Slept at night in a dog kennel*
> *But nobody chained him up.*

The simplicity here seems quite unaffected, and 'art' has
entered without any suspicion of aesthetic depersonalisation.
But what comes naturally to Dylan Thomas, and even
Eliot, does not to Auden, who is too naturally a craftsman,
a lover of the contrived and the urbane, to write successfully
in this sort of way. The conscious artist being determinedly
awkward is an embarrassing spectacle. Not that Auden's
attitude to real people, and especially the thwarted and mal-
adjusted whom he so often writes about, is in the least super-
cilious, clinical, or merely professional: those who criticise
the tone of his later poetry on this ground, and lament the
superseding of his occasional early uncouthness, are confusing technique and emotional sincerity. The latter is not

necessarily endangered by the former's search for new idioms and a new stylisation of insight. Artifice need not mean coldness of heart. And Auden is very much a new type of aesthete, who sees art not as religion but as a game, to be played with as skilful and individual a touch as possible. Consequently, while the above poem, with its raw uncertainty of touch, has curiously little flavour of Auden, these characteristic manipulations of the same type of experience could only have been written by him.

> The spring unsettles sleeping partnerships,
> Foundries improve their casting process, shops
> Open a further wing on credit till
> The winter. In summer boys grow tall
> With running races on the froth-wet sand,
> War is declared there, here a treaty signed;
> Here a scrum breaks up like a bomb, there troops
> Deploy like birds.   (Paid on both sides.)

> . . . To find those clearings where the shy humiliations
> Gambol on sunny afternoons, the waterhole to which
> The scarred rogue sorrow comes quietly in the small hours. . . .
>
>   (The Sea and the Mirror.)

>   In the soft-footed
>   Hours of darkness when elevators
>   Raise blondes aloft to bachelor suites
>   And the night-nurse notices a change
>   In the patient's breathing, and Pride lies
>   Awake in himself too weak to stir
>   As Shame and Regret shove into his their
>   Inflamed faces, we failures inquire
>   For the treasure also.   (The Age of Anxiety.)

There is a difference between these *Paysages Moralisés*, to borrow the ti.le of a poem, and the 'voluntary movements' which Auden so well describes, those vivid apprehensions of place and mood particularly common in the early poems, and of which we gave some examples at the beginning of this chapter. The latter are heavy with an emotional charge, usually of dread or expectancy, but they do not specify.

> *Beams from your car may cross a bedroom wall,*
> *They wake no sleeper; you may hear the wind*
> *Arriving driven from the ignorant sea*
> *To hurt itself on pane, on bark of elm*
> *Where sap unbaffled rises. . . .*
>
> (*Poems* 1930, No. 11.)

The former are abstract because explicitly meaningful: Auden has come more and more to rely, where social comment is concerned, on depersonalisation and the bird's-eye view, and when his landscape is not that of nostalgia or myth but is 'moralised' he prefers it to be allegorical and distant. This method can be highly effective—

> *Without are the shops, the works, the whole green county*
> *Where a cigarette comforts the guilty and a kiss the weak.*
>
> (Oxford.)

> *. . . long dead grandeurs whence the interest has absconded,*
> *As Fahrenheit in an odd corner of great Celsius' kingdom*
> *Might mumble of the summers once measured by him.*
>
> (*Commentary*.)

—but it can also be tiresome in the repetition of such phrases as *borough of murder, village of the heart, the ruined château of his faith, the squares of his mind.*

He is not, in fact, a master of that easy expository style

which is often attributed to him, and which he himself so much admires in a writer like Dryden—'the master of the middle style', as he calls him—and which is so useful for setting out some abstract point of view. Of recent years Auden has seemed increasingly to attempt the versification of a 'point of view'—usually a humanistic and Christian comment or gloss on some aspect of life today—and his success, insofar as he attempts 'the middle style', is not very great. The outlook that harmonises the complex activity of nostalgia and ritual daily goings-on cannot manage a lucid flow of explanation: an idea becomes clogged with irrelevant images which would be the making of a poem of mood or atmosphere, but which, when the idea is in any case expressible in prose sentences, merely get in the way. As an example of this the poem *Culture* is worth quoting in full, because it shows how the ingredients which are often the secret of Auden's earlier manner can confuse a more direct approach.

Happy the hare at morning, for she cannot read
The Hunter's waking thoughts, lucky the leaf
Unable to predict the fall, lucky indeed
The rampant suffering suffocating jelly
Burgeoning in pools, lapping the grits of the desert,
But what shall man do, who can whistle tunes by heart,
Knows to the bar when death shall cut him short like the cry of
*   the shearwater,*
What can he do but defend himself from his knowledge?

How comely are the places of his refuge and the tabernacles of his
*   peace,*
The new books upon the morning table, the lawns and the after-
*   noon terraces!*
Here are the playing fields where he may forget his ignorance

To operate within a gentleman's agreement: twenty-two sins have
    here a certain licence.
Here are the thickets where accostant lovers combatant
May warm each other with their wicked hands,
Here are the avenues for incantation and workshops for the cun-
    ning engravers.
The galleries are full of music, the pianist is storming the keys,
    the great cellist is crucified over his instrument,
That none may hear the ejaculations of the sentinels
Nor the sigh of the numerous and the most poor, the thud of
    their falling bodies
Who with their lives have banished hence the serpent and the
    faceless insect.

The idea here, that culture is a sort of cushion against the
existentialist horror of our predicament, maintained at the
silent expense of the inarticulate masses, is quite clear, but
its impact as a poetic statement has singularly little force. It
is a far cry to the exuberant urgency of *Consider this, and in
our time*, though the mechanism of the two poems does not
seem very different. The reason perhaps is that an *idea* rather
than a *mood* forms the poem's starting-point: Auden's mood-
dictated imagery is useless as expository illustration. We remember how he emphasises that the great contribution of
Yeats to modern poetry is the power to 'reflect' vigorously
and colloquially in verse that is never pedestrian. But Yeats's
method is very different.

> *Surely among a rich man's flowering lawns,*
> *Amid the rustle of his planted hills,*
> *Love overflows without ambitious pains;*
> *And rains down life until the basin spills,*
> *And mounts more dizzy high the more it rains*
> *As though to choose whatever shape it wills*

And never stoop to a mechanical
Or servile shape, at other's beck and call.

Mere dreams, mere dreams! Yet Homer had not sung
Had he not found it certain beyond dreams
That out of life's own self-delight had sprung
The abounding glittering jet; though now it seems
As if some marvellous empty sea-shell flung
Out of the obscure dark of the rich streams,
And not a fountain, were the symbol which
Shadows the inherited glory of the rich.

(Ancestral Houses.)

Here again the idea is plain enough, but it is dynamically in action, strengthened and coloured by the images. In fact neither image, neither fountain nor sea-shell, is necessary to Yeats's argument, but by affecting to find the second more accurate and choosing it in preference to the first, he gives most artfully the impression that this is an integral part of what he wants to say, that he is reflecting and expounding in images, correcting and refining as he goes along. Auden, on the other hand, proceeds with an apparent randomness from image to image: they jostle each other unselectively, distracting the reader, and piling up variations instead of revealing (or appearing to reveal) the stages of an idea. Alternatively he does without images altogether, and the sentiments then make even less of an impact.

That reason may not force us to commit
That sin of the high-minded, sublimation,
Which damns the soul by praising it,
Force our desire, O Essence of creation,
To seek Thee always in Thy substances,
Till the performance of those offices

> *Our bodies, Thine opaque enigmas, do,*
> *Configure Thy transparent justice too.*
> > *(In Sickness and in Health.)*

It is the taut conversational metre of Yeats, and so infectious
is metre that the poem even echoes some of Yeats's most
characteristic assertions,

> *The decorative manias we obey*
> *Die in grimaces round us every day,*
> *Yet through their tohu-bohu comes a voice*
> *Which utters an absurd command—Rejoice.*
> > *(In Sickness and in Health.)*

Apart from this semi-technical existentialist use of the word
'absurd', we are naturally reminded of *The Gyres*:

> *What matter? Out of cavern comes a voice,*
> *And all it knows is that one word 'Rejoice'!*

But Auden has much more difficulty than Yeats in convert-
ing his ideas and his exploration of theology, etc., into a
poetry that is at once conversational and eloquent. None the
less, in his latest collection, *Nones*, the problem does seem to
be getting solved. *Secrets*, with its long linked succession of
subordinate clauses kept perfectly in control until the main
verb descends with precision in the sixteenth line, succeeds
where a poem like *Culture* failed.

> *That we are always glad*
> *When the Ugly Princess parting the bushes*
> *To find out why the woodcutter's children are happy*
> *Disturbs a hornet's nest, that we feel no pity*
> *When the informer is trapped by the gang in the steam-room,*
> *That we howl with joy*
> *When the short-sighted Professor of Icelandic*

Pronounces the Greek inscription
A Runic riddle which he then translates,

Denouncing by proxy our commonest faults as our worst;
That, waiting in his room for a friend,
We start so soon to turn over his letters,
That with such assurance we repeat as our own
Another's story, that, dear me, how often
We kiss in order to tell,
Defines precisely what we mean by love:—
To share a secret.

The grammatical sequence holds the images together: and in place of the early exuberant dread, Auden is cultivating with great success a kind of lucid musing urbanity—the 'dear me' is engagingly characteristic of this new manner. And the manner is as effective when the *aperçu* of the poem is not Auden's own, but a recognised theme of perception which he is developing, as in <u>Memorial for the City</u>, where the opening section clearly illustrates Goethe's comment on the impassive and amoral universe of Homer.

The eyes of the crow and the eyes of the camera open
Onto Homer's world, not ours. First and last
They magnify earth, the abiding
Mother of gods and men; if they notice either
It is only in passing: gods behave, men die,
Both feel in their own small way, but She
Does nothing and does not care,
She alone is seriously there.

The crow on the crematorium chimney
And the camera roving the battle
Record a space where time has no place.
On the right a village is burning, in a market-town to the left

The soldiers fire, the mayor bursts into tears,
The captives are led away, while far in the distance
A tanker sinks into a dedolant sea.
That is the way things happen; for ever and ever
Plum-blossom falls on the dead, the roar of the water-fall covers
The cries of the whipped and the sighs of the lovers
And the hard bright light composes
A meaningless moment into an eternal fact
Which a whistling messenger disappears with into a defile:
One enjoys glory, one endures shame;
He may, she must. There is no one to blame.
The steady eye of the crow and the camera's candid eye
See as honestly as they know how, but they lie.

The images—favourites of Auden—lead up to the climax in an order both rational and graphic, and the poem continues as methodically as a nineteenth-century epic. Its subject is imposed from without; it has not grown up involuntarily within the poet as his earlier ones so clearly did; but whereas in even such successful transitional poems as *Musée des Beaux Arts* and *Voltaire at Ferney* this external quality has a slick finish which is a little too assertive and final, in the *Nones* poems it is both intense and sober, indicating a real maturity.

Maturity and an increasing interest in technique go together—not that Auden was ever uninterested in technique, but in *Nones* and *The Age of Anxiety* we find him experimenting with new devices in a far more patient and purposive manner than before. In *Poems* and *Look Stranger!* he availed himself in a casual way of Wilfred Owen's carefully used assonances: sported a frequent but equally haphazard use of the type of alliteration that controls Old English poetry (*A polar peril, a prodigious alarm*, is a good example), and was fond of a sort of Nordic shorthand that often lapsed comically into pidgin English—

> *Yet sometime man look and say good*
> *At strict beauty of locomotive,*
>
> > *(Poems* 1930, No. 16.)

—but at its best had a compelling literalness rare in the later poetry,

> *And recent particulars come to mind;*
> *The death by cancer of a once hated master,*
> *A friend's analysis of his own failure,*
> *Listened to at intervals throughout the winter*
> *At different hours and in different rooms.*
>
> > *(Poems* 1930, No. 16.)

In the *Letters from Iceland* he writes with admiration of the ingenuity of Scaldic metres and the verbal tricks of Norse poetry, and a late poem like *Pleasure Island* shows how much he learnt from it.

> *What there is as a surround to our figures*
> > *Is very old, very big,*
> *Very formidable indeed; the ocean*
> > *Stares right past us as though*
> *No one here was worth drowning, and the eye, true*
> > *Blue all summer, of the sky*
> *Would not miss a huddle of huts related*
> > *By planks, a dock, a state*
> *Of undress and improvised abandon*
> > *Upon shadowless sand. . . .*

The eye may miss at first the internal rhyme scheme on the penultimate vowel, but its regularity has established itself before we have read far, and is as effective in determining the mood of the poem—one of boredom, demoralisation, and concealed panic—as are the very different half-rhymes of Wilfred Owen's *Strange Meeting*. Auden is no longer slapdash. But such regularity has its own dangers—it may come to produce a poetry that 'does the poet's thinking and writing for him', as Goethe put it, a substitute for any deeper movement and expansion of the poet's mind.

It might be supposed that *The Age of Anxiety*, with its clever but continuous employment of Old English alliteration, is open to this danger, and that its technique is a mask for absence of development at a deeper level. But as we have seen, the whole question of 'development' where Auden is concerned can be referred to the difference between his attitude to poetry and his attitude to life. As with every romantic poet the compulsions that first drove him to write poetry are not such as his mature self can necessarily approve, but they remain the ineluctable source of vitality, to be disciplined perhaps—as technique disciplines them in the *Age of Anxiety*—but not to be superseded. Auden's first fascination was to make a myth out of the everyday, to join by the links of private connection the symbols that excited and intrigued him. In *The Age of Anxiety* this process is still going on: indeed it reaches its climax and its masterpiece. By taking the internal dialogue of four people and conveying it in a single style—the common style, one might say, of the fantasy life, with its mixture of fear and nostalgia—Auden has achieved a feat comparable to that of Virginia Woolf in *The Waves*. On the basis of the plays written in collaboration with Isherwood he has been criticised for failing to show at all realistically character exercised by dramatic situations, but in the *Age of Anxiety* he does something much more unusual: he shows us the desire of four people, at a time of

178

stress, to fall back on a sort of communal privacy of inner experience. In the seven stages of their fantasy journey there is ample scope for that exuberance of particularity in which Auden has always revelled. Quant the tired widower, Malin the intellectual doctor, Rosetta the Jewish business woman, Emble the handsome youngster accustomed to sexual success —all reflect with equal insight upon their different predicaments. A lifetime has taught Quant about the unexpected—

> *Unknown to him, binoculars follow*
> *The leaping lad; lightning at noonday*
> *Swiftly stooping to the summer-house*
> *Engraves its disgust on engrossed flesh,*
> *And at tea-times through tall french windows*
> *Hurtle anonymous hostile stones . . .*
> *We are mocked by unmeaning; among us fall*
> *Aimless arrows. . . .*

Emble voices the uncertainty of youth,

> *To be young means*
> *To be all on edge, to be held waiting in* ·
> *A packed lounge for a personal call*
> *From Long Distance, for the low voice that*
> *Defines one's future. The fears we know*
> *Are of not knowing. Will nightfall bring us*
> *Some awful order—Keep a hardware store*
> *In a small town. . . . Teach science for life to*
> *Progressive girls—? It is getting late.*
> *Shall we ever be asked for? Are we simply*
> *Not wanted at all?*

(Auden is fond of the metaphor of 'receiving orders' about one's destiny in life. Caliban in *The Sea and the Mirror* says that in reality—as opposed to art—'Time is not the dear old

179

buffer so anxious to please everybody, but a prim magistrate whose court never adjourns, and from whose decisions, as he laconically sentences one to loss of hair and talent, another to seven days' chastity, and a third to boredom for life, there is no appeal.')

But this reflection on experience is dwarfed by the day-dreams of the characters—their real defence against the un-happiness which all, in their varying ways, are acutely aware of. These fantasies provide a defence against chaos—the aim-lessness of life which Quant in particular feels—and give the poem its unexpected quality of zest and cheerfulness. Em-pirically at least, what emerges from the poem is that the remedy against Anxiety is the slightly absurd richness of the human consciousness, its capacity for protecting itself with a colourful cocoon of myth and invention. All this is very English—one is again reminded of Dickens—and the desire to make a satisfying pattern of the trivia of the consciousness comes out in such contradictions as the wish of Quant—or his creator—to find in or impose upon existence an exciting if sinister orderliness—(*Unknown to him, binoculars follow / The leaping lad*)—and yet his comment that 'We are mocked by unmeaning'. In fact our instinct is to repel the impression of unmeaning by some such inner game as Auden describes—

For the clear voice suddenly singing, high up in the convent wall,
The scent of elder bushes, the sporting prints in the hall,
The croquet matches in summer, the handshake, the cough, the
kiss,
There is always a wicked secret, a private reason for this.

(*Songs*, No. 3.)

In *The Age of Anxiety* these unheroic, gossipy, nostalgic tendencies of the individual in the solitude of himself are portrayed in a remarkably tender and moving fashion. The air of intellectual superiority that sometimes marred Auden's earlier expositions of the pathos and the vagaries of the private life has quite disappeared. The young Emble, uncertain, but complacent of his power to charm, is exposed without malice,

> How nice it feels
> To be out ahead: I'm always lucky
> But must remember how modest to look.

Most touching of the four is Rosetta, who conceals the memory of her real home and her unpresentable father by dreaming to herself of an imaginary childhood,

> In the housekeeper's room
> Was currant cake and calves'-foot jelly
> As we did our sums while down below,
> Tall in tweeds on the terrace gravel,
> Father and his friends reformed régimes,
> Moneys and monarchs, and mother wrote
> Swift and sure in the silk-hung saloon
> Her large round letters. . . .

She indulges in a fantasy of Gracious Living and big houses in 'one of those lovely innocent countrysides familiar to all readers of English detective stories':

> There was Lord Lugar at Lighthazels,
> Violent-tempered; he voted against
> The Banking Bill. At Brothers Intake
> Sir William Wand; his Water Treaty
> Enriched Arabia. At Rotherhope
> General Locke, a genial man who
> Kept cormorants. At Craven Ladies
> Old Tillingham-Trench; he had two passions,

Women and walking-sticks. At Wheels Rake
In his low library loving Greek
Bishop Bottrel; he came back from the east
With a fat notebook full of antique
Liturgies and laws, long-forgotten
Christian creeds occluded within a
Feldspar fortress. Fay was his daughter;
A truant mutation, she took up art,
Carved in crystal, became the friend of
Green-eyed Gelert the great dressmaker,
And died in Rome. There was Dr Sykes
At Mugglers Mound; his monograph on
The chronic cough is a classic still;
He was loved by all. At Lantern Byepew
Susan O'Rourke, a sensitive who
Prayed for the plants. They have perished now; their
Level lawns and logical vistas
Are obliterated; their big stone
Houses are shut.

She remembers, or rather invents, dolls that she once had, and the thought recalls her to reality.

Mocking blows the wind
Into my mouth. Oh, but they've left me.
I wronged. Then they ran. I'm running down.
Wafna. Wafna. Who's to wind me now
In this lost land?

For a poet with the reputation of being tough and impersonal Auden can produce effects of the purest romantic pathos, and with all its bizarrerie and wit, the poetry of Rosetta is perhaps the most moving he has written. An earlier hint of it, curiously similar in kind, is the fragment originally recited by the mad woman in *The Dog beneath the Skin*.

> *Seen when night is silent,*
> *The bean-shaped island*
> *And our ugly comic servant*
> *Who was observant.*
> *O the veranda and the fruit*
> *The tiny steamer in the bay*
> *Startling summer with its hoot—*
> *You have gone away.*

The action of the poem is deliberately and ludicrously inconclusive. The four characters meet in a bar; significantly, because Auden's description of what it offers is very like his view of what art offers—'an unprejudiced space in which nothing particular ever happens, and a choice of physiological aids to the imagination whereby each may appropriate it for his or her private world'—and from which, at the poem's end, the four characters and ourselves are 'reclaimed by the actual world in which time is real and in which, therefore, poetry can take no interest.' After their preliminary talk in the bar, followed by the alcoholic dream-journey which they take together, the four return to Rosetta's flat, and the two older men soon make their excuses and depart, benevolently hoping that Rosetta and Emble, who have shown signs of attraction for one another, will now make love. But Emble has drunk too much and passes out, and Rosetta in her final speech dispels the daydream about herself in which she has moved.

> *He'll never let me*
> *Conceal from him the semi-detached*
> *Brick villa in Laburnum Crescent,*
> *The poky parlour, the pink bows on*

The landing-curtains, or the lawn-mower
That wouldn't work. He won't pretend to
Forget how I began, nor grant belief
In the mythical scenes I make up
Of a home like theirs, the Innocent Palace
Where his law can't look, the leaves are so thick. . . .
My poor fat father. How appalling was
Your taste in ties. How you tried to have fun,
You so longed to be liked. You lied so,
Didn't you, dad? When the doll never came,
When mother was sick and the maid laughed. . . .

'His law' reminds us of the real and implacable world which Auden so constantly opposes to the mirror world of art. We move from one to the other, and both are necessary to us: Rosetta's disillusionment, so perennial a romantic subject, will not be a permanent one. And the finale is by no means negating or pessimistic. For a short while the four have, as Auden puts it, 'succeeded in establishing a rapport in which communication of thoughts and feelings is so accurate and instantaneous that they appear to function as a single organism'—and in which 'our faith in the existence of other selves, normally rather wobbly, is greatly strengthened and receives . . . the most startling justifications'. Communication between humans is possible at favourable moments, and at these moments it at once supports and contrasts with our individual expedients for survival, absurd and irrational as these may be,

> *. . . for plainly it is not*
> *To the Cross or to Clarté or to Common Sense*
> *Our passions pray but to primitive totems*
> *As absurd as they are savage; science or no science,*

It is Bacchus or the Great Boyg or Baal-Peor,
Fortune's Ferris-wheel or the physical sound
Of our own names that they actually adore as their
Ground and Goal.

The upshot of the poem, then, is affirmative and curiously heartening, despite the pathos and futility it reveals. There is nothing knowing or pretentious in the poet's understanding: indeed, compared to such would-be 'definitive' poems as *Spain* or *Commentary*, *The Age of Anxiety* is curiously modest in tone. None the less, and perhaps partly for this reason, it remains Auden's greatest achievement to date, and the one which best shows the true nature of his scope and talent.

It is significant that it is dedicated to John Betjeman, and that Edmund Wilson should have expressed the opinion that Auden and Betjeman were the two most considerable English poets writing today. Whether or not one agrees with this verdict, it is true that no other two poets have made so much (though Betjeman's range is of course a great deal slighter) of the lyrical possibilities afforded by the contemporary scene; no two have made so vigorous and fascinating—and in Auden's case so capacious—a myth out of the way in which people, for better or worse, are actually living. The subject matter of their poetry approaches that of the modern novel—the social apparatus, solitude and the expedients for evading it, the vivid perceptions and totems of childhood, the details and personality of places and people —but it never loses the unique advantage which romantic poetry has: its ability to turn whatever it touches into mystery and charm.

CHAPTER X

Dylan Thomas

IN DISCUSSING Auden and Yeats we have not had much trouble with their language: we have been able to talk about their poetry, its style, the attitudes and preoccupations it reveals, without needing to consider in any detail its linguistic basis. Both poets can be obscure. But their obscurity rests on a sound referential structure which, like conversation or prose, can be understood by analysis or factual enquiry. *Byzantium* is a difficult poem because the images in Yeats's mind have a sequence and development which we cannot grasp all at once: a line in one of his last poems—

For since the horizon's bought strange dogs are still

is obscure until we discover that it refers to the purchase by Dorothy Wellesley of some land near her house on which stray dogs had formerly disturbed her with their barking. We may object to Yeats's employment of this private reference, but we cannot consider it impenetrable. Both Yeats and Auden often use words in a startling and unfamiliar way, but if we follow up our surprise we always find some coherent and external reason for the usage. Take Yeats's use of the word *bundle*—a favourite of his. Its homely violence always contrasts with something ceremonious and ordered; in *That the Night Come* he uses it to suggest the undignified but magnificent haste with which a king discharges the ritual of his marriage day, and this combination of magnificence with unselfconscious lack of dignity is precisely what he wants to suggest an aspect of Maud Gonne. Similarly, in *Parnell's Funeral*—

> *Under the Great Comedian's tomb the crowd.*
> *A bundle of tempestuous cloud is blown*
> *About the sky . . .*

the word associates with *Comedian* to convey the mingled absurdity and splendour of Parnell's fate. The word is the poet's: he has put his own particular stamp upon it. But on this high poetic level he uses it as coherently and consistently as ordinary speakers would use a word like 'cat' or 'anger'. Auden writes of the *lovers* who *warm each other with their wicked hands*. Why *wicked* hands? We are checked and intrigued for a moment, and the word's precision positively begs us to enter a complex of meaning which illuminates the poem's, and the author's, whole outlook. The juxtaposition with *warm* is part of the effect, as in *human on my faithless arm*: Auden is attached to such contrasts. A less obvious and more moving use of the same type of pregnancy occurs in Keats's sonnet—

> *The moving waters at their priestlike task*
> *Of pure ablution round earth's human shores,*

By altering *cold* in the first draft of the sonnet to *pure*, Keats gives the epithet *human* a new significance; the two adjectives, each inconsiderable by itself, lend each other meaning. One of the most striking examples of this kind of poetic pregnancy is Valéry's use of the word *scrupuleux* for the course of a small stream among pebbles. By suggesting both the delicacy and the difficulty of the water's progress around stones, and by returning to the original sense of scruple as pebble, the word in this context combines the fullest traditional sense with the surprise of a new application of it. The same sense of language is implied in Herrick's famous phrase 'the tempestuous petticoat', which T. E. Hulme singled out as showing the kind of 'zestful accuracy' that he thought all poetry should have.

But though poetry can achieve it with such effect, this kind of meaningfulness is not by any means confined to poetry. It is simply the aesthetic use of words, the careful and conscious employment of them for the sake of the rich mental movements and apprehensions that underlie them. We have the feeling of penetrating beneath the surface of language to the thought, and returning to repose upon the quality of the word: the word as a thing and the word as an indicator are in perfect accord, and as thing the word has an absolute appeal which is none the less connected with its referential function. Used in this way, language seems, to borrow a philosopher's distinction, simultaneously opaque and transparent—it both *is*, and reveals. It seems probable that all poetic language attempts by its very nature this impressive dual function; and since critics of poetry have become semantically conscious, various formulations of the dualism have been made—language used affectively or logically, emotively or cognitively, as 'soundlook' or as reference.* All these distinctions are perhaps ultimately misleading, but they do serve to indicate, with shifting degrees of emphasis, the freedom of language on the one hand, and its attachment to given phenomena and the rational linking of them, on the other.

* For these and similar distinctions see Vendryes: *Le Language*. I. A. Richards: *Principles of Literary Criticism*. Elizabeth Sewell: *The Structure of Poetry*. So far as I know, the distinction between opaque and transparent poetry was first made in the context of a different argument by Stephen Spender in *Poetry for Poetry's Sake*. (*Horizon*, No. 16.)

Poets as well as critics have become self-conscious about the linguistic side of their craft. The surrealists attempted to run the two aspects of language together, and to make words as things in some way achieve the whole effect of poetry. That, at least, was what they hoped would happen. In practice it seems doubtful whether the mind, with its habitual conditioning to word→ thought can ever be persuaded to repose solely upon the word as thing: quite involuntarily it will start upon some referential chain-reaction, even though—in the determination of the poet to thwart it —this may be of a baffled and abortive kind. The old romantic technique of 'suggestion' merely amounted to casting the net of reference in a wider and more subjective arc, and letting the reader's mind swim indolently in pursuit of whatever it brought up: the new technique of surrealism attempted to startle the reader's mind into stopping at the word. Other and earlier departures in poetic language, like those of Rimbaud and Hopkins, tended to have the same effect, though this may not have been the writer's intention —it was far from being that of Hopkins. None the less, in a poem like *Harry Ploughman* we seem to be unable to get away from the words to their subject,

> *Hard as hurdle arms, with a broth of goldish flue*
> *Breathed round; the rack of ribs; the scooped flank; lank*
> *Rope over thigh; knee-nave; and barrelled shank—*

But at least we know what the subject is: and though the words are so obtrusive the description they add up to is quite simple, as simple as in the highly referential descriptions of W. H. Auden, like that quoted on page 151. In surrealist poetry there is, almost by definition, no such cohesion: each word is at war with its neighbour, and syntax is systematically dislocated in the effort to make language a thing, a structure, on its own. Often we feel that in such poetry enormous pains are being taken to make language pregnant in the manner indicated by our examples from Yeats, Auden, and Keats. And the attempt seems doomed to failure, for the reader's mind desperately pursues the references set in motion by the impact of each word, and is denied the normal cohesion of subject or syntax which give him a firm hold in even so 'wordy' a poem as *Harry Ploughman*.

The poetry of Dylan Thomas has obviously much in common with that of Rimbaud and Hopkins, and with the word expedients of conventional surrealism as well. Any attempt to interpret and appreciate it, therefore, should perhaps start from the standpoint of language: we are most likely to find what Thomas is getting at, what he wants to say, if we first examine the linguistic forms in which he has been driven to say it.

Words, single words, are far more important in Thomas's poetry than in that of Yeats or Auden. We should expect this. Although Auden has said that a 'passionate love of words' is a pre-requisite for every poet, his own highly referential language depends much more on that 'natural momentum of syntax' which Yeats sought for so diligently, than on the individual word. The norm of both Yeats's and Auden's poetry is fluency, conversation: the norm of Thomas's is incantation, the single word as thing, dropped on to the page. Keeping in mind this basic distinction, we might seek a first foothold on the difficulties of Thomas's poetry by a comparison of some of his adjectives with those referential ones whose operation we have already discussed.

(1) *Socket and grave, the brassy blood,*
    Flower, flower, all all and all.

(2) *Forged in man's minerals, the brassy orator*
Laying my ghost in metal. . . .

(3) *My Egypt's armour buckling in its sheet,*
I scrape through resin to a starry bone
And a blood parhelion.

(4) *Turning a petrol face blind to the enemy*
Turning the riderless dead by the channel wall.

(5) *Where once the waters of your face*
Spun to my screws

(6)   . . . *the nitric stain*
On fork and face.

(7) *The night is near,*
A nitric shape that leaps her, time and acid;

(8) *On field and sand*
The twelve triangles of the cherub wind
Engraving going.

(9) *My veins flowed with the Eastern weather;*
Ungotten I knew night and day.

(10) *Consider now the old effigy of time, his long beard*
whitened by an Egyptian sun, his bare feet watered
by the Sargasso sea.

(11) . . . *So fast I move defying time, the quiet gentleman*
Whose beard wags in Egyptian wind.

(12) *In the poles of the year*
When black birds died like priests in the cloaked hedge row
And over the cloth of counties the far hills rode near.

(13) *Once it was the colour of saying*
Soaked my table the uglier side of a hill
With a capsized field where a school sat still
And a black and white patch of girls grew playing.

(14) *The chitterlings of a clock* . . .

(15) *Though the town below lay leaved with October*
blood.

(16) *My busy heart who shudders as she talks*
   Sheds the syllabic blood and drains her words.
(17) *The puffed birds hopping and hunting, the milkmaids*
   Gentle in their clogs over the fallen sky.

If we analyse the individual words in these extracts we are
puzzled by the wide variation of effect which they reveal.
Some show the poetic pregnancy, simultaneously existing as
satisfying 'thing' and as subtle indicator, which we expect in
more straightforward poetry. In extracts 8 and 12 all the
words—*cloth, cloaked, cherub*—have this quality, and engraving combines smoothly and comprehensibly the sug-
gestions of the wind furrowing snow or sand, and the lines
etched in relief on a sundial's face (it is an obvious truth of
romantic poetry that exact words usually 'suggest' far more
powerfully than vague ones). *Chitterlings* is as surprising as
Valéry's *scrupulous,* and as effective. *Puffed* in 17 is similarly
exact, and *syllabic* in 16 suggests both the prophetic touch
of *sibyl* or *sibylline* and is also a language metaphor comparable to 'the reasons of the heart'. *Leaved with October
blood* is a simple conceit or metaphor for autumn leaves, as
is *the fallen sky* for snow-covered ground. *Capsized* in 13 is
a more purely metaphysical usage that would have delighted
Shakespeare or Donne; the pun has a lyrical wit, and the
precision of the verbs *sat* and *grew* indicates the blend of
repose and restless movement which haunts Thomas's vision
of adolescence. 5 is similarly a metaphysical conceit. 4, 10,
and 11 are examples of a private but coherent and consistent
image, like Blake's star and tiger; *Egyptian* and *eastern* are
always images of time for Thomas. *Nitric* and *brassy* are
more puzzling: *nitric* again seems to have associations for
Thomas of time and wearing away, but its use in the second
instance is confusing, though the word *acid* gives a kind of

dislodged clue. *Brassy* as applied to orator is clear enough, but what is its relation to blood, and why *starry* bone? Language here seems to have left the referential for the absolute pole; sign has become thing, and such faint referential echoes as we can catch are necessarily uncertain, and do not lead us with any inevitability. A *parhelion* we find, on consulting the dictionary, is 'a spot on a solar halo at which the light is intensified . . . a mock sun'. We look in vain here for any metaphysical clue; Thomas does not appear to use the word as a meaningful illustration, like Donne's intelligences and spheres, but for its sound, and its exotic unfamiliarity. A stock Romantic usage in fact, such as one might find in Swinburne, or, in a rather different way, in Yeats. *Riderless* is tolerably easy: again the associations are romantic—Riders to the Sea, the riding ship,—the phrase is as eloquent for the dead here as it is for the unborn in the line,

A limp and riderless shape to leap nine thinning months.

And it reminds us of one of the most beautiful of all Thomas's compressed epithets, *the riding Thames*, in the poem *A Refusal to Mourn*, which gives the feeling of the river's immortality as a part of the child's death.

But the phrase *a petrol face* is implacably opaque. In this context the word does not seem alive at all, though the questing associative faculty might revolve the images of the sea bird *petrel*, or of the stain of oil on top of the water. I suspect, though, that the very inertia of the word may be the reason for its presence here: after a succession of 'live' words (e.g. 'the *haring* snail' in the preceding stanza), the intrusion of a 'dead' one may be the effect intended—the closest parallel that language can offer for an actual physical apprehension of death.

Though they are not the most complex that could be

found in his work, these examples, particularly the last, do give us, I think, a sense of the issues involved, and of how devious and varied is the task which Thomas sets to the resources of language. They help to explain, too, the bewilderment and frustration which even the most careful and devoted reader cannot help feeling on occasion. Scarcely has he accustomed himself to one kind of linguistic usage—say the conventional exactness of *capsized field*, or *blood-counting clock*—when he has to adjust himself to an entirely different one. It is as if the attitudes to language of Donne, Blake, and Swinburne were all to be encountered in the same poem. The revival of interest in metaphysical technique has left its mark on Thomas, and he is not the only modern poet in whom the task of 'prehending language emotionally and intellectually at once' (the comment is Auden's) imposes a severe strain upon the reader. In her book on the imagery of the Metaphysicals,* Miss Tuve has suggested that one secret of the strength and clarity of their poetry is that their images omit 'all but the one prick of the point of connection' which the sense requires. In other words, where a true metaphysical use of language is concerned, in such a phrase as

> *Age is love's timber, youth his underwood,*

we are not to dwell upon either the 'thingy' or the associative nature of the words *timber* and *underwood*, but simply to grasp the meaning towards which they point as metaphors. In a romantic use of language, the significance of the words as metaphors would be weak or vague, and their suggestive power correspondingly dwelt upon. The reaction of the modern poet—and it is a very understandable one—is, why not have both? Indeed, William Empson, in a review of Miss Tuve's book,† ques-

---

* Rosamond Tuve, *Elizabethan and Metaphysical Imagery*.
† *Kenyon Review*, 1949.

tioned whether this insulation of imagery could exist, and implied that to write or to read poetry as if it could was to impoverish the scope of poetic effect. 'If you can't explain what seems to you a good line and still decide to print it you are trusting that the reader has the same feelings as yourself.' The use of the word 'feelings' here is obviously suspect: Empson makes use of a romantic terminology which is out of place in speaking of Metaphysical poetry in the historical sense. Donne would not have appealed to his readers' feelings to decide on the decorum of an image which seems to us to do inexplicably more than indicate a metaphorical connection—he would have appealed to their wit and reason. The answer is perhaps that the insulation process may take place if the reader is linguistically habituated to it: and making associations in poetry is equally a habit rather than a necessity, as is sharing the 'feelings' of a poet who has let a line stand although he cannot explain it. All readers who are brought up on romantic poetry find difficulty in appreciating the native qualities of the Metaphysicals, and are tempted to extract from them whatever seems to fall in with their own habits of reading: historically speaking we can be fairly sure that the reading habits of the poet's audience in the seventeenth and the nineteenth centuries were in fact very different. But now we are being asked to combine the two. If our tastes are eclectic, and we are seasoned in all sorts of poetry, this should be ideal, but it can only happen effectively if all the poem, and the images in it, can be read both 'metaphysically' and 'romantically'. Problems will occur if some of the poem seems to show metaphysical 'sense' and other parts associational 'sound', or some other type of linguistic effect. And this, as our examples show, does occur in Thomas's poetry.

The result is a degree of warring, and sometimes damaging, comparison. It is only with great agility and understanding that the reader can accept such varying usages as each functional and necessary in its kind: the tendency at first is to react sharply to the 'transparent' and referential clues, and gloss helplessly over the more opaque and difficult words and passages. In consequence the wholeness of the poem remains difficult to grasp; it is as if—to adopt a rough-and-ready metaphor—our progress through it was not a smooth expanding flow, but rather an obstacle race at different levels—scrambling over objects, falling into holes, and clambering painfully out again to nerve ourselves for a jump across a chasm or a tightrope walk between two trees. In the course of this uneven journey the reader has the right to ask himself whether Thomas's use of language is not simply good at some points and bad at others; whether, in fact, the whole procedure is not a hit-or-miss method based on the elementary use of poetic 'pregnancy' which we discussed at the beginning of the chapter; and in which Thomas is a careless genius often blessed with good luck, instead of a laborious craftsman obsessed with the ways in which language can be brought more and more directly into contact with feelings and things.

I believe that the second view is the right one, but it is a difficult thing to demonstrate. The critical uncertainty which must still be felt about Thomas's real status as a poet arises from the fact that we still do not know whether language is capable of what he tried to do with it; or rather whether the consciousness of the receiver can adapt itself to such a variety of linguistic uses and such a multiplicity of verbal stimuli. Probably it can. In its necessary evasion of a *status quo*, language in its aesthetic uses is always tending to become more complex, to demand a greater degree of vigilance and delicacy in its apprehension. Acting, as it does, as a kind of mirror of the trained self-consciousness, it is always seeking to enlarge that consciousness, to force upwards into the light of its expression the inchoate mass of vague awareness which lies below the level of thought and speech. Thanks to theoreticians like Freud and Jung, the degree of self-consciousness which we have already attained about our submerged selves is remarkable, perhaps frightening—one wonders where such exploration is going to end, if not in a blank limbo of unfruitful understanding. The language of poetry can perhaps act, in a strange way, as a kind of vitaliser of such understanding, as a means to keep it alive and kicking. Although, by its very nature, poetic language is bound to turn feeling into thought (as an early surrealist remarked, *La pensée se forme dans la bouche*—words must become thoughts in order to be words), when the process takes place in poetry we retain the mysteriousness and the joyfully hidden quality which existed before the transformation; the sense of thoughts that do lie too deep for words, even though —by some miracle—we are reading those words on the printed page. Poetry can thus act not only as an enlightener —and Thomas often spoke of his obsession with making dark things clear and plain—but as a corrective to enlightenment, as a means of combating the sterile progress of self-consciousness. In his autobiography Arthur Koestler tells a story of a woman with a mental disorder who had hallucinations: she had been much analysed and knew exactly what the significance of her visions was in terms of childhood hates, sex fears, etc., and she accepted with a dreary finality the accuracy of the interpretation; but it gave her no help, and as her visions persisted the lucidity with which she could now objectify them brought her nothing but despair, in spite of the affirmatory and liberal tone which her Jungian analyst attempted to impart to the enlightening process. The bringing of the hidden to light by poetry is a very different order of experience, requiring not a ready-made general vocabulary, but its own fibre of thought and language which appears—even though this may be an illusion—to have been dragged up from the same depths as the experience itself.

This exploration and bringing to light of the dark interior, the 'unknown modes of being', was once the primal Romantic aim, the chief preoccupation of Wordsworth and Coleridge. Although any comparison of these two with Thomas would obviously, at this stage, be ridiculously premature, it is probably true that no other poet since them has shared their interests so much as he. Although we cannot tell as yet what size of poet he is (and he may yet be judged as intrinsically slight as Laforgue or Clare or Owen), yet he has the absorption and the single-mindedness of the great Romantics. He shows the same steady inward gaze as Wordsworth, the same inspired egotism, but whereas Wordsworth attempted to trace the growth and movements of his mind in the plain lucid diction which he thought proper to poetry and which he had in fact inherited from the eighteenth century, Thomas tries to get at the mystery of his own growth and being by means of his own highly personal idioms and image clusters. Not that Wordsworth's language—so far as its effect on the reader is concerned—is like the normal language of rational intercourse or prose. As F. R. Leavis has pointed out, although Wordsworth's meditation appears to be 'preoccupied with a scrupulous nicety of statement', its overall effect is in fact largely independent of this semblance of analysis. It wakens—to borrow Shelley's phrase—'a sort of thought in sense': its conventionality of detail leads the reader on to perceptions of a deeper, non-rational kind. And this process has one enormous advantage which Thomas's poetry conspicuously lacks. When it is necessary for Wordsworth to make some direct statement, to link the stages of his poem by some purely intellectual armature, he can do it without any incongruity and without any obvious switch to a different order of understanding. He can, to put it baldly, draw a moral in the same language in which he has conveyed a vision. Moreover he can attempt to relate his own personal experiences to the general social background, because there is nothing in his language which is inapplicable to such a background: it is one of the great strengths of Wordsworth's and Coleridge's Romanticism that they admit no division between the hidden depths they explore, and the human situation in its widest and most social sense.

It is worth illustrating this point by means of a famous passage from *The Prelude*. In the passage in Book Twelve beginning 'There are in our existence spots of time . . .' Wordsworth tells how one of his chief 'visitings of imaginative power' befell him when he was lost on a stretch of lonely moor where a gallows had once stood. Running away in panic he sees a girl with a pitcher on her head.

> *It was, in truth*
> *An ordinary sight; but I should need*
> *Colours and words that are unknown to man,*
> *To paint the visionary dreariness*
> *Which, while I looked all round for my lost guide,*
> *Invested moorland waste and naked pool,*
> *The beacon crowning the lone eminence,*
> *The female and her garments vexed and tossed*
> *By the strong wind. When, in the blessed hours*
> *Of early love, the loved one at my side,*
> *I roamed in daily presence of this scene,*
> *Upon the naked pool and dreary crags,*
> *And on the melancholy beacon fell*

A spirit of pleasure and youth's golden gleam;
And think ye not with radiance more sublime
For these remembrances, and for the power
They had left behind? So feeling comes in aid
Of feeling, and diversity of strength
Attends us, if but once we have been strong.
Oh! mystery of man, from what a depth
Proceed thy honours. I am lost, but see
In simple childhood something of the base
On which thy greatness stands; but this I feel,
That from thyself it comes, that thou must give
Else never canst receive. The days gone by
Return upon me almost from the dawn
Of life: the hiding-places of man's power
Open; I would approach them, but they close.
I see by glimpses now; when age comes on,
May scarcely see at all; and I would give,
While yet we may, as far as words can give,
Substance and life to what I feel.

The transitions here between the naked event described, and the commentary on it, are masterly. The retrospection (and Wordsworth's finest poetry is almost always avowedly retrospective) does not in the least detract from the shock and thrill of the experience, and the impact that it makes on the reader. There is a breadth and humility in his attitude which reaches its climax in the calm simplicity of that *I am lost*, all the more effective for being in no way gestured about or dwelt on—indeed a hasty reading might overlook it. In two places Wordsworth explicitly disclaims the efficacy of language to render what he felt: the poetry is not only retrospective but an admitted paraphrase. None the less it comes to us directly. Even the impersonal, unstressed diction (the bleak *female* which was substituted for *woman* in the 1805 edition) has its share in the impression: and the phase which trembles on the verge of cliché, 'A spirit of pleasure and youth's golden gleam', contrasts with the 'visionary dreariness' to render the mysterious interrelation between terror and happiness—even a light, conventional happiness —which the poet discerns.

Now, the experiences that Thomas tries to bring to light are not very different from these, but he has none of Wordsworth's social and retrospective breadth. Perhaps he does not want it. He is writing in a poetic climate about which Auden, as we have already noted, remarked in 1927—'Emotion is no longer necessarily to be analysed by "recollection in tranquillity": it is to be prehended emotionally and intellectually at once.' It is this arduous synthesis that Thomas is unconsciously trying to achieve, and the absence of retrospection in his poetry—its unswerving truth to what is going on rather than to what *has* gone on—throws considerable light on its linguistic difficulty. The counterpart to our embarrassment over the different ways in which he uses words, the different 'meanings' he imposes on them, is the way in which darkness and light, experience and explanation, are often present together in the same poem, but in an unfused state: when synthesis fails the poem is troubled (in a way Wordsworth's can never be) by the obscurity of its direct 'stuff' and the comparative banality of an emergent gloss or commentary on it. Sometimes, in fact, we suffer a positively uneasy feeling when Thomas *is* clear. Is this what all the business is about? is our reaction. When the poem, instead of being taken in at some deep, almost wordless, level of the mind, brings itself to the rational surface, it loses its lustre like a stone from a rock pool exposed to the air. Working the whole movement of a poem at different levels is as difficult and dangerous a feat as using words in different ways and with different kinds of emphasis. Discrepancies in the poem's wholeness are almost inevitable.

This explains, too, the contrast between the rich unlimited feel of some of his poems, and the startlingly finite nature of others—a contrast which has led to the conclusion of some critics that Thomas had very little 'to say', and that when he had, in a muffled but compelling manner, got it out, there remained nothing for him to fall back on but the virtuosity with words which he had acquired in the process. Poems like *The Hand that Signed the Paper, This Side of the Truth, We Lying by Sea Sand, The Hunchback in the Park*, have this finished quality, as of a perception well handled and expertly rounded off, which would be quite in keeping with the bent of Auden or even—to take a very different example—W. H. Davies, but which do have an effect of incongruity in the context of Thomas's work. Versatility is oddly disturbing in a poet whose strength and linguistic originality seem to lie in a kind of inspired *groping*—'groping for matter under the dog's plate'. And this groping delicacy—it is one of the things that make it so good when it works—teeters continually on a knife-edge between complete opacity and the inertia of ordinary 'sense'. To appear to be striving after sense, as Thomas sometimes does, to be saying something with difficulty which is simple enough to be said in an approximate form with ease—that is a nemesis which his linguistic approach cannot always avoid. Consider the first two stanzas of *Out of the Sighs*.

> *Out of the sighs a little comes*
> *But not of grief, for I have knocked down that*
> *Before the agony; the spirit grows,*
> *Forgets, and cries;*

A little comes, is tasted and found good;
All could not disappoint;
There must, be praised, some certainty,
If not of loving well, then not,
And that is true after perpetual defeat.

After such fighting as the weakest know,
There's more than dying;
Lose the great pains or stuff the wound,
He'll ache too long
Through no regret of leaving woman waiting
For her soldier stained with spilt words
That spill such acrid blood.

The hesitant, rather awkward statement of the first stanza, with its marked absence of images, makes its point circuitously, almost timidly: 'A little', something positive, something worth having, emerges from the sadness and the impoverishment of growing up, of living; even unhappy love supports this positive residue. In the next stanza the point is developed. Our reaction to the wounds of life is to retain this as it were reservoir of feeling, of neutral contentment or grief, which is indifferent to the original conflicts and causes—the 'woman waiting'—and which is in some way associated with the poet's capacity to name what has happened to him, to put it into words. The association of words with blood and feeling—the mention of them in the same breath and as if they were the same order of things—is characteristic of Thomas and we must return to it: it is worth comparing it here with the conventional statement of Wordsworth that words, a different method of perception, can only be put alongside what he once felt, as an approximate description.

The poem continues:

Were that enough, enough to ease the pain,
Feeling regret when this is wasted
That made me happy in the sun,
How much was happy while it lasted,
Were vaguenesses enough and the sweet lies plenty,
The hollow words could bear all suffering . . .

Were that enough, bone, blood, and sinew,
The twisted brain, the fair-formed loin,
Groping for matter under the dog's plate,
Man should be cured of distemper.
For all there is to give I offer:
Crumbs, barn, and halter.

'The little' now emerges more clearly as that neutral over-plus of vitality which makes one 'happy in the sun'; if this state of equilibrium, which the poet now connects with 'vaguenesses' and 'sweet lies', were enough for living, then words—which inhabit this province—would be more powerful than they are. *Hollow* suggests not only impotence but the rounded, protected state, succeeding effort and grief, in which words operate. Words here *are* being looked at as something retrospective, and this seems to conflict with their position in the preceding stanza: as the stress of the poem develops the point of view has perhaps changed. Certainly the referent of *enough* appears to modify in the last stanza—it is now the naturalness of man, the instinctiveness in him which cannot be hurt by his emotions. Yet the modifications are easy enough to follow and do not disturb the poem's comparatively simple idea. The tone of the poem seems to ask to be understood in the same cerebral way, but almost as if Thomas felt how uncertain and indefinite his attempt at this kind of explication was, he rounds it off with

two lines which, though startlingly inconsequential, do give
a sudden vigorous jerk to the poem's ending. What they
mean in the context of the poem is another matter: it is
tempting to suppose that their vigour is their function and
that the matter ends there. Perhaps the poet is stressing again
how little words, poetry, can give: perhaps the final line
should be followed out exactly—crumbs of consolation; a
place to rest and also to store strength and experience; a
voluntary dedication or servitude which may finally be (by
the association of halter with hanging) an instrument of
death and despair. These are what words may bring. But I
have no confidence that the reader is intended to pursue
these crossword clues of association: they may be simply
misleading, and my tentative exegesis of the poem may bear
no relation to the impression other readers may get from it.

The uncertainty here is crucial, because it is the result of
Thomas's eclectic employment of language. When the
poetry does not succeed in synthesising these employments,
and imposing its own absolute illusion of confidence, the
reader simply does not know what to do. Is he to receive a
general impression, as from a Shelley lyric? Or is he to
pursue all the implications of language as meticulously as he
would in a poem by Pope or Donne? Both these kinds of
poetry have their own confidence, their own ability to carry
the reader with them, but an apparent hesitation between
them in the poet makes for a complete bewilderment in the
reader.

I think we must conclude that on these grounds *Out of the
Sighs* does not come off as a poem, not because it sets too
difficult a task to the reader (for as we have seen the emergent idea seems simple enough) but because it leaves him in
doubt about the way to read it. Many instances of this, in
poems or in parts of poems, can be found in Thomas. In the

205

poem *I, in my Intricate Image* we are again confronted with an idea, almost a conceit, in the first line of the poem,

I, in my intricate image, stride on two levels,

but in the ensuing stanzas, despite the references to *two, twin,* and so on, we cast about helplessly for a coherent development of this idea—

Forged in man's minerals, the brassy orator
Laying my ghost in metal,
The scales of this twin world tread on the double,
My half ghost in armour hold hard in death's corridor
To my man-iron sidle.

Beginning with doom in the bulb, the spring unravels,
Bright as her spinning-wheels, the colic season
Worked on a world of petals;
She threads off the sap and needles, blood and bubble
Casts to the pine roots, raising man like a mountain
Out of the naked entrail.

Beginning with doom in the ghost and the springing marvels,
Image of images, my metal phantom
Forcing forth through the harebell,
My man of leaves and the bronze root, mortal, unmortal,
I, in my fusion of rose and male motion,
Create this twin miracle.

Tread, hold, and *sidle* must all have the same relation to the sentence of the first stanza as verbs—'my half-ghost in armour holds hard in death's corridor to my man-iron, and sidles (towards it)' would presumably be the grammatical sense rendering. It is difficult to see why the sentence should be malformed, and why the two appearances of the poet should both be armour-clad, man in iron and ghost in iron.

The images then change abruptly to that thick physical vision of spring rising in man and nature which is one of Thomas's obsessions. At the end of stanza three we look in vain for a connection between the restatement of this 'twinness' theme—now seen as a 'fusion of rose and male motion', and the original image of man and ghost in armour. Further images follow, and in the last stanza of the first section of the poem the armoured couple are seen as invalids in a sanatorium,

> Intricate manhood of ending, the invalid rivals,
> Voyaging clockwise off the symboled harbour,
> Finding the water final,
> On the consumptives' terrace taking their two farewells,
> Sail on the level, the departing adventure,
> To the sea-blown arrival.

'On the consumptives' terrace taking their two farewells' might almost be a line from Auden, but the image of sickness and departure is bewilderingly unlike what has gone before. It hints at a quite different and more accurately controlled image world, like an equally surprising line in the poem *On No Work of Words*.

> To surrender now is to pay the expensive ogre twice.

Expensive ogre, invalid rivals, indicate briefly an ordered system of metaphor unlike Thomas's own. He is as eclectic in his images as in his words, and quite often they have a literary, as opposed to a personal and individual, origin. His frequent use of the phrase *Death's Feather*, for example, though it no doubt refers to the custom of holding a feather to the lips of the dying to see if they still breathe, may also derive from a recollection, I think, of the lines in T. S. Eliot's poem *A Song for Simeon*.

My life is light, waiting for the death wind,
Like a feather on the back of my hand.

All this does not make the reader's task any easier. In *Out of the Sighs* the poet seemed to be reaching towards an idea that could be expressed in fairly simple language: In *I, in my Intricate Image* he resigns the poem to a welter of images, none of which exercises any authority over its neighbours.

My images stalk the trees and the slant sap's tunnel,
No tread more perilous. . . .

In this poem, too, the difficulties do not succeed in resolving themselves. The assistance in the composition of harmony that a master-image would give is expressly rejected by Thomas, and this is perhaps the moment to give his own views on the subject, as they were very illuminatingly set forth to Henry Treece.

It consciously is not my method to move concentrically round a central image. . . . A poem by myself needs a host of images. I make one image—though 'make' is not the word; I let, perhaps, an image be made emotionally in me and then apply to it what intellectual and critical forces I possess—let it breed another, let that image contradict the first, make, out of the third image born out of the other two together, a fourth contradictory image, and let them all, within my imposed formal limits, conflict. Each image holds within it the seed of its own destruction, and my dialectical method, as I understand it, is a constant building up and breaking down of the images that come out of the central seed, which is itself destructive and constructive at the same time. . . . I do not want a poem of mine to be, nor can it be, a circular piece of experience placed nearly outside the living stream of time from which it came; a poem of mine is, or should be, a watertight section of the stream that is flowing all ways, all warring images in it should be reconciled for that small stop of time.*

Two things in this account are of particular interest to us. First, the concept of warring and contradictory images, by which I take it that Thomas means images not only in conflict with each other but of a different kind from each other. As described the process has a kind of impressive formality about it, like Hegel's triadic dance, but one cannot help wondering if it does not sound more convincing in theory than it may work out in practice. Secondly, the avowed absence of retrospection: 'a circular piece of experience placed nearly outside the living stream of time from which it came' would be an accurate enough description of Wordsworth's poetic method. Thomas, on the contrary, wants to achieve the equivalent of the 'stream of consciousness' in prose fiction, to give the feeling of words rising instantaneously from the lapse and flow of consciousness. There is in fact a direct connection between time and language as Thomas conceives them; instead of following, and as it were making a retrospective comment on the shapelessness of consciousness, Thomas's language attempts to be part of the flow. Not that this implies facility: changing the metaphor completely in another comment on his poetry, he speaks of it as 'not flowing' but rather 'hewed out' from the intractable material of his mind. The implied admission that the poem, though it may appear to be 'a watertight section' from the flux of time, is really composed as laboriously as the poetry of any more conventional craftsman, shows how difficult a task Thomas has set himself in 'making a momentary peace with the images at the correct moment'. Such a peace does not occur in the inchoate surge of thought and

* Henry Treece: *Dylan Thomas* (Lindsay Drummond).

feeling inside the mind: it must be imposed from without, while at the same time the illusion of time's flow in the receptive mind must be retained, and it is not surprising that the trick of this does not always come off.

When it does, we are no more conscious of the conflict of disparate images which—so Thomas tells us—have gone to make the poem, than we are when we read any other kind of Romantic poem—*Kubla Khan* for example. Moreover, Thomas is often at his most successful when he is as much *outside* the poem as we are—when he is *telling* us what he is feeling and doing, instead of obscurely *doing* it; when, in fact, the poet seems at a conventional remove from his poem, like the craftsman from his material. It is for this reason that the early poem *Especially when the October Wind* is one of the finest of Thomas's achievements. The 'outsideness' here is most marked, and it takes the form of the poet's identifying the languages he uses with the objects he so vividly perceives. A kind of external convention is produced, in which the poet formally attaches the terminology of language— *Vowelled, wordy, syllabic, signature, speeches, signs*—to the world of nature—water, women, birds, and so forth.

> *Shut, too, in a tower of words I mark*
> *On the horizon walking like the trees*
> *The wordy shapes of women, and the rows*
> *Of the star-gestured children in the park.*
> *Some let me make you of the vowelled beeches,*
> *Some of the oaken voices, from the roots*
> *Of many a thorny shire tell you notes,*
> *Some let me make you of the water's speeches.*
>
> *Behind a pot of ferns the wagging clock*
> *Tells me the hour's word, the neural meaning*
> *Flies on the shafted disk, declaims the morning*

And tells the windy weather in the cock.
Some let me make you of the meadow's signs;
The signal grass that tells me all I know
Breaks with the wormy winter through the eye.
Some let me tell you of the raven's sins.

Especially when the October wind
(Some let me make you of autumnal spells,
The spider-tongued and the loud hill of Wales)
With fists of turnips punishes the land,
Some let me make you of the heartless words.
The heart is drained that, spelling in the scurry
Of chemic blood, warned of the coming fury.
By the sea's side hear the dark-vowelled birds.

With the aid of this convention—and though brilliantly idiosyncratic it is really as straightforward as Yeats's calculated terseness or Wordsworth's impressionistic lucidity of diction—Thomas does achieve in these early poems an objective identification of his subject matter with the language in which he describes it. The convention is, I think, the key to these poems' success and originality of impact. It is an unadmitted convention: it has nothing to do with the dialectical war and peace of images in which, as we have seen, Thomas later came to envisage the theoretic process of a poem. But it has much to do with the gap between word as thing and word as sign, and the still greater gap between language and the actuality of blood, growth, procreation—the obsessional subject-matter of the poems. It is a method of bridging—or appearing to bridge—these gaps, and its operation has the supreme advantages of clarity and order—we see what is happening and are compelled by it. There is no doubt here, as there is elsewhere in Thomas, about how we are to react to this phraseology: it is self-explanatory, and gives the impression—common in more conventional poems that come off—that the poem is in some way a *prelude* to the poetic experience which it will arouse in the reader: it carries us along with it, moved but unquestioning, to its close, and it is then we begin to wonder about the nature of the words that have been said to us, and to analyse them. While the poet is talking we listen: when he has finished we ask questions. It is this order of response which is lacking when Thomas tries to telescope the process, and to make his experience as poet in some way coexistent with our experience as reader. In poems like *Out of the Sighs* and *I, in my Intricate Image*, the linguistic stages of examination, narration, and response are jumbled together—our groping reaction is uncomfortably simultaneous with Thomas's groping approach, and we feel that the attempt to jump the gaps of language and feeling has not succeeded. The attempt there seems fundamentally unaesthetic and doomed to failure. We might compare it with Thomas's use of the word *petrol* in the line

Turning a petrol face blind to the enemy

which I have already commented on. If I am right in supposing that *petrol* is there purely because its inertness as a word corresponds to the meaningless inertia of death—Thomas might presumably have said *apron* or *bamboo* or *income* to get the same effect, if those words happened to possess a comparable euphony—the whole aesthetic function of language as a search within formal limits and rules, for the right, the nicely indicative word, is threatened with breakdown. Similarly, if the mental stages underlying the formulation and response to language—the sequence of coherence —is ignored, it is difficult to see why words should be used at all. The logical end would be Mallarmé's sheet of blank paper, or the self-imposed silence of the more extreme surrealists.

When Thomas's desire to bring words and experience closer together is successful, therefore, it succeeds through the use of a convention in no way different from the type of convention of which poets have always made use. He speaks of words, blood, women, in the same breath, and with the same almost terrifyingly intense awareness of their *existence*. It is an awareness of everything as vocal, as talking to him as he talks himself. 'The spider-*tongued*, and the *loud* hill of Wales.' For Thomas, not only is seeing a language, as Coleridge remarked: *being* is a language too. It is a highly personal use of a metaphor—the pathetic fallacy Ruskin called it—which poetry has always possessed. Skies have always wept in poetry, trees moaned, blood been eloquent. But Thomas's apprehension of this metaphor is far more acute and ordered than that of any previous poet. He is conscious of language as

> *the voice that, like a voice of hunger,*
> *Itched in the noise of wind and sun.*

In the poem *I Fellowed Sleep* he writes:

> *Then all the matter of the living air*
> *Raised up a voice, and, climbing on the words,*
> *I spelt my vision with a hand and hair. . . .*

The senses are compressed and interchanged—*matter* of the air, a voice *itching*, thoughts *smell* in the rain. This synaesthesia gives the abstractness of thought and language the almost overpowering reality of Thomas's physical apprehensions like

> *Some dead undid their bushy jaws,*
> *And bags of blood let out their flies,*

or

> The bagpipe-breasted ladies in the deadweed
> Blew out the blood gauze through the wound of
> manwax.

He speaks of the *supper and knives of a mood*, and in the later
poems the convention is still kept up, with phrases like
oyster vowels, meat of a fable, wick of words. Thomas is haunted
by the indivisibility of mind and matter. The throat is where

> Words and water make a mixture
> Unfailing till the blood run foul . . .

and the brain, he says,

> was celled and soldered in the thought
> Before the pitch was forking to a sun.

The *shapes of thoughts*—a perfect phrase for Thomas's use of
words—and the *declension of the flesh* constitute a kind of extended organic metaphor in Thomas's poetry. *Man be my
metaphor* he ends one poem, and he tries to convey that the
speaking function of man, so far from being a civilised accomplishment and overlay, is as deep and mysterious as his
unconscious instincts. Even the sea does not elude the language metaphor in which Thomas invests creation and gives
it order. In a note about his poems—and his prose vocabulary
has all the characteristics of his poetry—he speaks of the
unparagraphed sea.

Of course this metaphoric structure is not the explanation
of the poetry's power—many other factors are involved as
well. Most notable of these is Thomas's skill in juxtaposing
sounds, vowels and consonants, to produce an almost physical impact. His oral vigour is amazing—one would scarcely
believe that English was capable of it—and depends for its

complete effect upon an un-English fullness of articulation, the kind of articulation which Thomas gave to his reading. Consider the movement of *some dead undid their bushy jaws,* and the X and Z sounds between the long U's in *Blew out the blood gauze through the wound of manwax.*

> *And I am dumb to mouth unto my veins*
> *How at the mountain spring the same mouth sucks.*

The effectiveness of sound as a part of sense does not need to be laboured. It is a traditional part, a function of language as 'thing', which has always been used as an adjunct to poetic meaning, and is quite different from the attempt, which Thomas sometimes seems to be making, to get sound and referential pointlessness to carry language closer to mood and feeling. His poetry, as in the examples just quoted, often both means and sounds physically: the sensation is that we are being assaulted by some means other than words. And this again shows how powerful is the double use of language in his poetry. If I read the sentence: 'He came at her with a knife', I may shrink from the scene conjured up by its meaning, if I am a sensitive person, but this reaction will be caused by the words as indicators, not as things. Even an apparently strenuous couplet of Auden's,

> *And mobilise the powerful forces latent*
> *In the infected sinus and the eyes of stoats . . .*

though it seems at first to resemble Thomas in its insistence on physical detail, will be found, I think, to operate almost entirely referentially if we compare it to Thomas's

> *her threadbare*
> *Whisper in a damp word, her wits drilled hollow,*
> *Her fist of a face died clenched on a round pain,*

or

> *The swing of milk was tufted in the pap,*

where the 'thinginess' of language seems to flourish alongside its sense, and is deliberately courted as an accessory to
physical references. In this, as in so much else, Thomas has
revived rather than invented. We find the effect in Pope,

> *. . . Alum styptics with contracting power*
> *Shrink his thin essence like a shrivelled flower—*

where the physical thinness of the words is a part of their
total meaning, and—with a fullness of vowels like Thomas's
own—in Keats,

> *Then glut thy sorrow on a morning rose,*
> *Or on the wealth of globed peonies. . . .*

I return to insist on the importance in Thomas's poetry of
this dual function of language, because the peculiar use he
has made of it will perhaps be his chief claim to distinction.
At a time when the language of poetry has seemed to be in
danger of being pulled apart between the meaningless
exuberance of surrealism on the one hand, and the self-conscious precision of poets influenced by positivistic theory on
the other, he has achieved a balance between the two, in his
best poems, while retaining—and even drawing our attention to—the separateness of both. It is because of this separateness that his poetry does not lend itself to analysis in terms
of its content. Indeed we can go so far as to say that whenever such analysis is possible, and seems desirable, the poem
has not been a success. A prose paraphrase, such as those
attempted by Julian Symons, and made the basis of an adverse verdict on the poems, is clearly no sort of critical lever
at all. Except on rare occasions—as in *Out of the Sighs* and

The Hand that Signed the Paper—even an attempt to say what Thomas's subject is only leads to misunderstanding and to a shrinking of the poem's true dimension.

This is not to say that any criticism of the poetry must be of a purely negative kind, though I think that indication of the types of linguistic experience we encounter in his work, and of how we may best enjoy them, remains the most constructive critical approach. One more positive evaluation that may be made, however—and this is also closely bound up with his linguistic practice—is of the way in which he achieves the effect of compression in time, the physical reality of 'in my beginning is my end' which of all Thomas's special apprehensions is the one most powerfully conceived and carried out. We must remember here our earlier remarks on his symbolism. Thomas's awareness is never expressed 'symbolically' when it conveys this prehension, but always with absolute literalness: he himself said that he wished his poetry to be taken literally, and at its best—as when this kind of awareness is involved—it always can be. There is no gap— no intellectually sensible gap that is—between our grasping of the words and our deduction of what they are supposed to stand for. It is this gap which is the nemesis of so much poetic symbolism, and when it does not occur it is perfectly accurate to speak of the poem or part of the poem as 'literal'. In this sense Blake's poem *O Rose Thou art Sick*, is literal, and so is Thomas's *Twenty-four Years*.

> *Twenty-four years remind the tears of my eyes.*
> *(Bury the dead for fear that they walk to the grave in labour.)*
> *In the groin of the natural doorway I crouched like a tailor*
> *Sewing a shroud for a journey*
> *By the light of the meat-eating sun.*
> *Dressed to die, the sensual strut begun,*

With my red veins full of money
In the final direction of the elementary town
I advance for as long as for ever is.

We do not need to ask what this poem is *about*. It means what it says, and the line *In the groin of the natural doorway I crouched like a tailor* does not refer to the concept of birth any more than Blake's *Invisible worm that flies in the night, in the howling storm* refers to an abstract idea of evil, energy, the male principle, etc. A symbol in poetry, if it works, might be defined as a literal statement which can be apprehended so clearly that this very shock of apprehension conveys other possibilities of meaning. We can apprehend it, but not explain it, for, in the words of Wittgenstein, 'that which expresses *itself* in language we cannot express by language'. The secret of the symbol's power to set the mind at work is its initial confidence, vigour, and absorption in itself. This is why the literalness of a fairy story often seems to mean more than it says, or lines like,

> *The Queen was dressed in scarlet*
> *Her merry maids all in green—*

Or Thomas's own,

> *And there this night I walk in the white giant's thigh.*

Thomas's own comment on a poem of his, criticising Edith Sitwell's analysis of some lines in it, is very illuminating.

> *Altarwise by owl-light in the half-way house*
> *The gentleman lay graveward with his furies;*
> *Abaddon in the hangnail cracked from Adam,*

And, from his fork, a dog among the fairies,
The atlas-eater with a jaw for news,
Bit out the mandrake with tomorrow's scream.

Of the last two lines Edith Sitwell commented: 'they refer to the violent speed and the sensation-loving, horror-loving craze of modern life'. Thomas remarked that this was very vague. 'She doesn't take the literal meaning: that a world-devouring ghost creature bit out the horror of tomorrow from a gentleman's loins.' This is certainly literal and graphic enough, but the thought strikes us, could not Edith Sitwell's interpretation follow from this literal meaning? Isn't her meaning legitimate for her, and for anyone else whose feelings and preoccupations happen to be ignited in the same way by the lines? Does an insistence on literal meaning, in fact, save us from the ensuing welter of subjective reactions? The answer is, perhaps, that a literalness of the graphic and absolute kind indicated by Thomas (and Edith Sitwell does seem to have ignored the castration image that the syntax uncompromisingly insists on) should preclude any vagueness of response, such as ideas about the speed of modern life, etc. A graphic, unambiguous statement should never produce a vague suggestion. But the opposite of vague here is not clearly formulated. As Arthur Symons wrote in his essay on Maeterlinck: 'All art hates the vague; not the *mysterious*, but the vague: two opposites very commonly confused.' Whatever we get from Thomas's lines will not be easy to express, but it will, or should, be controlled by the literal violence of his words which pin down our response to certain kinds of actuality. The reason why poetic symbols (as we have seen in the case of Yeats) are often vague and dreamy is because there is less discrepancy between the images and the impressions we get from them; the creator's unconscious reasoning seems to be: impressions from poetry are inchoate, therefore let the words and sentences that produce them be the same. 'O world! O life! O time!'— Shelley's poem invites the vaguest and most ethereal possible response. But as we have said, the inchoate is not necessarily vague, nor is it abstract. The movement in the mind of words like *fork, jaw, scream, bit,* is sufficiently forcible to prevent the journey from the words themselves to parallel abstractions about them. We are back here at the linguistic problem with which we started: the alternative (admittedly an oversimplified one) of stopping at the words or penetrating into the thought behind them. If the thought can only appear, like Edith Sitwell's version of it, at an unwarrantable remove from the words, we are unwise to seek for it. *Search* for Thomas's meaning is a dangerous process; we may have to read a passage carefully to discover its literal meaning, but, once discovered, there should be no further conscious search for a concealed significance; Thomas's own gloss on the extract gives an indication of how the literal meaning can be followed up rather than interpreted. 'The mouth of the creature (the Atlas-eater) can taste already the horror that is not yet come, or can sense its coming, can thrust its tongue into news that has not yet been made, can savour the enormity of the progeny before the seed stirs, can realise the crumbling of dead flesh before the opening of the womb that delivers the flesh to tomorrow.'

The lines, in fact, show Thomas's obsessional theme, the telescoping of existence—'Time held me green and dying'. And we shall find it whenever we look behind the words. That is why we may feel a sense of disappointment and limitation if we are continually looking for an idea, and may prefer—as Edith Sitwell evidently preferred—to suppose that Thomas is making some kind of poetic comment, about 'modern life'. Another critic's interpretation of the first stanza of *When, like a Running Grave.*

> *When, like a running grave, time tracks you down,*
> *Your calm and cuddled is a scythe of hairs,*
> *Love in her gear is slowly through the house,*
> *Up naked stairs, a turtle in a hearse,*
> *Hauled to the dome,*

—suggests that the image of the dead turtle-dove taken to the skull means 'when love is intellectualised'. Apart from the fact that turtle-dove, though poetic, receives no warrant in the text—the grotesque side of Thomas and the word *haul* indicate a more conventional turtle—the idea of 'intellectualising' is a concept at an immense distance from the words: we cannot move from the words towards such a hypothetical idea at the back of them without doing violence to the actuality of the poem. Granted that the image is puzzling, it seems likely that once again the subject is the coincidence in time of birth, love, and death—the image of going upstairs is used more than once in Thomas to indicate this process, as in *The Conversation of Prayer,*

> *. . . the man on the stairs*
> *Who climbs to his dying love in her high room . . .*
> *And mark the dark eyed wave, through the eyes of sleep,*
> *Dragging him up the stairs to one who lies dead.*

And the reference to skulls in the later stanzas of *When, like a Running Grave* indicates the death aspect of the theme traditionally enough ('to this favour must she come') without any need to suppose that Thomas is concealing with images *ideas* about the nature of love.

None the less, the poet himself is partly to blame. If we are confused and baffled by a literal reading, it is difficult not to cast about for some explanation or 'message' contained in the poem. Literalness is often not forcible enough for us to recognise its implications without trying to interpret it. Thus Professor Olson suggests that *The Ballad of the Long-legged Bait* 'deals with the possibility of salvation through mortification of the flesh'. The implication is that Thomas is writing a mediaeval allegory, a kind of *Piers Ploughman*, or at least a poem with the moral structure of *The Ancient Mariner*, whereas the comparison should rather be with, say, Rimbaud's *Bateau Ivre*—both poems are a vision of life rather than the treatment of a problem in life. Where the symbolic is concerned, and in Thomas in particular, energy can often act as a kind of substitute for clarity. It was Yeats who first employed symbols in English in the energetic style, and Thomas's most successful poems display the same characteristic. In *Twenty-four Years*, for example, the energy of the poem carries us through without a halt. The only word which might give us pause is *elementary*, where we should expect *elemental*, but the reason for it is partly euphony, to avoid a repetition of the *al-* sound two lines back; and partly —one imagines—to get the shock effect of peeling off the normal associations of a commonplace word to reveal its basic meaning. The compressed violence of the second line is contextual for Thomas: he echoes it infrequently—*In the groin's endless coil a man is tangled*—and *my father's ghost is climbing in the rain*, in phrases like *dressed to die*, and in *After the Funeral*—

> . . . *a desolate boy who slits his throat*
> *In the dark of the coffin and sheds dry leaves.*

It is at these moments, too, that the elevated and rhapsodic movement and tone, which the Welsh preachers and their audiences call *Hwyll*, is most marked. This uplifted but natural eloquence is scarcely heard at all today in English poetry—the kinds of self-consciousness which we have noticed in Eliot and Auden are an effective deterrent to it— and the movement of *After the Funeral*, with its unfaltering and yet disciplined exaltation, sends us back to the tradition of *Lycidas* and Spenser's *Daphnaida*.

A criticism often made about Dylan Thomas is that he did not develop, that his subject matter is purely himself, and that once he had brought out 'from darkness to light' the obscure matter which obsessed him, his poetic potentialities were exhausted. It is true that his poems are always, broadly speaking, about the same thing, and the most striking difference between his early and his later poems is the way in which what had been groping and shapeless, an exploratory movement continued from one poem to the next, takes on a closed and almost geometrical completeness of form. *From Love's First Fever to her Plague* has the same preoccupation with the unity of our bodily experiences in time—birth, copulation, death—as a late poem, *The Conversation of Prayer*. But the later poem, with its delicately handled scheme of inner rhymes, is intent on establishing an already known fact by technical means, by an aesthetic pattern, almost as the mood of Owen's *Strange Meeting* or Auden's *Pleasure Island* is determined by these means, while in the early poem the apprehension in the poet's mind has still to be explored and given provisional shape. But this shift from exploration to aesthetic presentation does not make *The Conversation of Prayer* any weaker than its predecessor: on the contrary, the later poem seems to me in every way better. To suppose that when a poet does not know what he wants to say before he begins writing the poem must necessarily be more compelling than when he does, is a dangerously absurd criterion; but in the case of Thomas it has often been implied. What is undoubtedly true of both poems is that they cover, each in its different way, the whole poetic experience of their author. There is nothing left over. No development of *ideas* can follow from them, just as it cannot follow from Sweeney's vision of life—

> *That's all the facts when you come to brass tacks*
> *Birth, copulation, death.*

But Sweeney reflects his author's horror at these 'facts', from which some kind of release must be found, which demand some sort of higher explanation; while for Thomas their simple existence is enough for poetry.

Nor, in Thomas's later work, is their existence apprehended only in the individual, in the poet himself. It might seem that his world was necessarily an enclosed one, a world of intuitions about the imprisoned self which could be shared between writer and reader but is not capable of demonstration in terms of the communal nature of man. *Under Milk Wood* shows that this is not the case. As Auden in *The Age of Anxiety* gives us a drama not of social relationships but of the interrelated fantasy life of four individuals, so Thomas presents society in terms of a day in a Welsh village, a day which is also a lifetime. His invariable vision, the jumble of death and life, is extroverted into a frieze of figures, young and old, male and female. The women gossip round the pump.

> Same as ever. Who's having a baby, who blacked whose eye, seen Polly Garter giving her belly an airing, there should be a law, seen Mrs Beynon's new mauve jumper, it's her old grey jumper dyed, who's dead, who's dying, there's a lovely day, oh the cost of soapflakes!

Polly Garter addresses her baby.

You're looking up at me now. I know what you're thinking, you poor little milky creature. You're thinking, you're no better than you should be, Polly, and that's good enough for me. Oh, isn't life a terrible thing, thank God?

The drowned speak to Captain Cat, the old seaman, who sails back into the past 'through the voyages of his tears'.

How's it above? Is there rum and laverbread? Bosoms and robins? . . . Fighting and Onions? . . . Washing on the line? And old girls in the snug? Who milks the cows in Maesgwyn? When she smiles, is there dimples? What's the smell of parsley?

In his imagination Mr Edwards addresses impassioned pleas to his beloved.

I am a draper mad with love. I love you more than all the flannelette and calico, candlewick, dimity, crash and merino, tussore, cretonne, crepon, muslin, poplin, ticking and twill in the whole Cloth Hall of the world. I have come to take you away to my Emporium on the hill, where the change hums on wires. Throw away your little bedsocks and your Welsh wool knitted jacket, I will warm the sheets like an electric toaster, I will lie by your side like the Sunday roast.

As the second quotation shows, Thomas does not avoid (indeed it is probably not his purpose to avoid) a certain coarsening here of the vitality which wells up so strangely in his poems. 'Isn't life a terrible thing, thank God' might indeed be a summing-up of the impression that his poetry leaves with us, but here it is too much a short cut, too arch an approximation, which reminds us uncomfortably of the 'wind on the heath, brother', Chesterton and Belloc style of affirmation. But though *Under Milk Wood* was intended specifically for a wireless audience such overt forcing of the atmosphere does not often occur: on the whole the play carries through its conviction of reality successfully by means of its separate characters. In becoming more 'popular' and giving his individual vision a social basis, Thomas puts himself in the tradition of vivid and colloquial fantasy which runs from Shakespeare and Congreve through Dickens to James Joyce, and he uses this tradition in the best sense, without sacrificing any of his own individuality. Mr Pugh, dreaming of poisoning his wife, is a figure who takes his place in an august line of English fantastics, but he is also pure Thomas.

> Alone in the hissing laboratory of his wishes, Mr Pugh minces among bad vats and jeroboams, tiptoes through spinneys of murdering herbs, agony dancing in his crucibles, and mixes especially for Mrs Pugh a venomous porridge unknown to toxicologists which will scald and viper through her until her ears fall off like figs, her toes grow big and black as balloons, and steam comes scream-ing out of her navel.

There are the same syllabic contrasts and concealed rhymes, but the language has become more consistently exact, its combination of 'thing' and reference more orthodox, with-out losing any of its vigour. It is done as engagingly as Rosetta's daydreams in *The Age of Anxiety* but with an undernote of physical reality and violence as graphic as the ghost's description of the poisoning in *Hamlet*. Phrases like *Samson-syrup-gold-maned,—she sleeps very dulcet in a cove of wool*—cows as *summerbreathed slaves walking delicately to the farm*—equally announce the fact that Thomas seems to have returned to the fold of conventional aesthetic language.

We can almost equate, then, Thomas's inclusion of society in his poetic vision with a return to tradition. If he had lived, his poetry might have continued to develop along the lines suggested by the 'public' subject of *Under Milk Wood*. The figure of Polly Garter in particular (we may remember Arnold's depression at the name and the idea of the accused woman Wragg) suggests that Thomas might have been able to create characters drawn from common life but living and breathing in poetry, instead of the characters with a poetic halo stuck artificially round them who inhabit contemporary poetic drama. Beginning in himself, Thomas's poetic apprehension, so absolute and so homogeneous, was beginning to turn outwards into the world of other human beings, seen as individuals going about their concerns. He had no need to create a world of myth out of this real world as did the other poets whom we have studied: its existence, like his own existence, would have been enough. He would have seen Man, as he had seen himself, 'up to his head in his blood', and—for that very reason—also up to his head in a world of poetry.

INDEX